Northwestern University
STUDIES IN *Phenomenology &*
Existential Philosophy

GENERAL EDITOR
John Wild

ASSOCIATE EDITOR
James M. Edie

CONSULTING EDITORS
Herbert Spiegelberg
William Earle
George A. Schrader
Maurice Natanson
Paul Ricoeur
Aron Gurwitsch
Calvin O. Schrag

Phenomenology of Willing and Motivation

Alexander Pfänder

Translated, with an Introduction

and supplementary essays by

Phenomenology of Willing and Motivation

and Other Phaenomenologica

HERBERT SPIEGELBERG

Northwestern University Press

1 9 6 7

Acknowledgments

I would like to acknowledge gratefully the following permissions for translation and reprinting:

(1) To Johann Ambrosius Barth Verlagsbuchhandlung, Munich, for the Introduction to the *Phänomenologie des Wollens* and the entire essay "Motive und Motivation," which appeared in the same volume of *Alexander Pfänder's Gesammelte Schriften* (3rd ed.; Munich, 1963), pp. 3–11, 125–55.

(2) To the Max Niemeyer Verlag Tübingen for the Introduction to *Logik* (3rd ed.; Tübingen, 1963), pp. 1–30.

(3) To Martinus Nijhoff, the Hague, for two texts from Herbert Spiegelberg, *Alexander Pfänder's Phänomenologie* (The Hague, 1963), pp. 36–40, 46.

(4) To Professor Adrian van Kaam, Duquesne University, for the article, "The Idea of a Phenomenological Anthropology and Alexander Pfänder's Psychology of Man," first published in the *Review of Existential Psychology and Psychiatry*, V (1965), 122–36.

(5) To the Universidad Nacional Autónoma de México, Mexico, for the article " 'Linguistic Phenomenology': John L. Austin and Alexander Pfänder," first published in *Memorias del XIII Congreso Internacional de Filosofía*, IX (1964), 509–17.

I am indebted also to the Committee on Faculty Research Grants of Washington University for aid in the preparation of the original manuscript of this book. In addition, I would like to acknowledge the ready and efficient help of the typing staff of the Department of Philosophy, Mrs. Marlene Hoffman, Mrs. Ruth Zimmermann, and Miss Lynn Dardick. Mr. Richard Holmes helped me greatly with the proofreading.

But my major debt goes to my friend, the late Bayard Quincy Morgan, emeritus professor of German at Stanford University, a master translator, who checked and streamlined my drafts and was both a stern and constructive critic of my own text. Without his prompt and unfailing help I would not have had the courage to go through with my undertaking.

H. S.

Contents

Translator's Introduction

[I] JUSTIFICATION

THE PRESENT VOLUME of translations from the works of Alexander Pfänder (1870–1941), published twenty-six years after his death, needs some explanation. Ever since I arrived in the United States in 1938, I have been wondering whether there was any possibility of (or, indeed, any reason for) introducing this practically-unknown older phenomenologist to the Anglo-American world. Quite apart from the precariousness of my own foothold at the time, I had serious doubts as to whether Pfänder's work was relevant to Anglo-American philosophy and psychology as I came to know them, with all their old and new resistances to the better-known phenomenologists and existentialists. In fact, in 1949, in a book review I had expressed the fear that it was both too late and too early to present Pfänder to English-speaking philosophers.[1] Had it not been for the surprising fact that Pfänder had fared so much better in the Spanish-American world, where two of his earlier works had been translated and were well-known, I might have abandoned all hope and saved myself a futile effort which easily could have been interpreted as mere sentimental piety toward one's former teacher.

All the same, when I finally was persuaded to try my hand at a general historical introduction to phenomenology, I made an attempt to give Pfänder his due place in the history of the movement, i.e., immediately after Husserl, and described his special version of phenomenology and recommended some texts for possible translation. But the first serious stimulus for such a translation came when Paul Ricoeur, one of the few French phenomenologists aware of Pfänder

1. "Philosophie der Lebensziele," *Philosophy and Phenomenological Research,* X (1949), 441.

[xv]

and his work, although he had never met him, mentioned his name repeatedly at the second Conference for Phenomenology at Lexington, Kentucky, and at the third meeting of the Society for Phenomenology and Existential Philosophy at Yale in 1964. It was Professor Adrian van Kaam of Duquesne University who then suggested to me that I translate Pfänder's essay on "Motive und Motivation." So, with the assistance of my friend Bayard Quincy Morgan, I now embarked on the translation of this essay. I had hardly completed it when the Northwestern University Press expressed interest in this piece for their "Studies in Phenomenology and Existential Philosophy." Its major fault turned out to be that it was too short for publication in the series. This objection finally gave me the chance to try to do what I really had wanted: to assemble a representative group of several texts from Pfänder's work which could test his potential significance for the Anglo-American public. The present realization of this larger plan still falls short of what seems to me eventually desirable—the translation of most of Pfänder's larger works. But at this time the more important thing is to provide access to those texts which have relevance to current needs and which give concrete illustrations of Pfänder's conception of a phenomenological philosophy.

[II] BIOGRAPHICAL DATA

A BRIEF SKETCH of Pfänder's development, against which the translated texts can be viewed, would seem to be in order. Alexander Pfänder, born in Iserlohn, Westphalia in 1870, studied first at the Engineering School in Hanover, where he absorbed a good deal of mathematics and science. Only after the completion of these studies did he discover in Theodor Lipps at the University of Munich a guide to philosophy and psychology. But though he soon became Lipps' leading student, he was never his follower. Lipps' psychology, in spite of its stress on pure description, disappointed him in comparison with the more penetrating view of the human psyche which he had found in Schopenhauer and Nietzsche. Moreover, along with many of Lipps' later students, Pfänder objected vigorously to his "psychologism," which made Lipps one of the prime targets of Husserl's classic attack in the *Logische Untersuchungen*.

Pfänder began his work in descriptive psychology with two studies on the psychology of the will: the first, his doctoral dissertation, was a critical piece; the second was a constructive one, which was awarded a university prize. It also served him as a qualifying thesis in 1900, when he became *Privatdozent* at the University of Munich, where he stayed until his retirement as full professor in 1935. The thesis appeared under the title *Phänomenologie des Wollens* (*Phenomenology of Willing*), a year before Husserl had adopted the term "phenomenology" for his new logical investigations in 1901. But the coincidence and similarity of their enterprises were sufficient to establish a momentous association after Husserl's *Logische Untersuchungen* had appeared and Husserl himself had paid a visit to the Munich group. Contacts with Husserl in Göttingen intensified and finally, in 1913, led to the establishment of the *Jahrbuch für Philosophie und phänomenologische Forschung*, in which Pfänder took an important part as a co-editor, especially in its early years. When Husserl's position moved from a descriptive phenomenology of essences to a transcendental idealism, Pfänder followed his course only slowly and partially. His first contribution to the yearbook, "Zur Psychologie der Gesinnungen," is still a piece of "eidetic" phenomenological psychology. His *Logik* of 1921, undertaken in response to Husserl's own request in 1906, shows a cautious adoption of some features of Husserl's phenomenology, stressing the role of subjective viewing. However, to Pfänder phenomenology was never more than a new approach to the central questions of philosophy. It was to these questions that he applied it in his lectures on "Introduction to Philosophy and Phenomenology," which he planned to develop for publication. Pfänder's crowning achievement remained his attempt at an interpretive psychology under the title *Die Seele des Menschen* in which, on the basis of an enlarged phenomenological conspectus of the human psyche and its life, he tried to determine their essential nature and their proper meaning or destination.[2] He was also close to completing a work on ethics, based on a phenomenology of value and oughtness (*Sollen*), which links it with his philosophical anthropology. His growing heart ailment, combined with discouragement over the general and philosophical situation in Nazi Germany, prevented the fruition of his publication plans during his remaining decade. Fragments can be found in the *Pfänderiana* collection, now deposited in the Bayerische Staatsbibliothek in Munich.[3]

Pfänder never exerted the influence on the philosophical scene which Husserl and, in a very different manner, Scheler and Heidegger did. But his Socratic stimulation affected a widening circle of younger

2. Cf. below, Herbert Spiegelberg, "The Idea of a Phenomenological Anthropology and Alexander Pfänder's Psychology of Man," Appendix A, pp. 75–85.

3. See also Herbert Spiegelberg, *Alexander Pfänder's Phänomenologie* (The Hague, 1963), Appendix.

colleagues and students, as evidenced, for instance, by a *Festschrift* commemorating his sixtieth birthday.[4] I shall refrain from adding to this evidence my personal testimony, as I did in my obituary of him.[5] Let me include two less biased pieces which only recently came to my attention.

One, a more general tribute to the Munich phenomenologists, stems from Nicolai Hartmann in a letter to Alexius Meinong, who had asked Hartmann in 1915 about his attachment to the *Phänomenologen* and particularly to Husserl. Hartmann's reply of September 28, 1915, contains the following sentences:

> My regard for this tendency is related almost exclusively to the younger phenomenologists, with whom in my estimate the method has become really alive and has penetrated the special questions for which it is made. Here I am thinking particularly of Geiger and Scheler, but also of Reinach, Pfänder, Leyendecker, and others.[6]

Specific references to Pfänder's *Logik* occur in Hartmann's first openly phenomenological work.[7]

The other piece of evidence turned up in the autobiography of one of the leading Munich historians, which contains the following passage about a lecture course by "a recently admitted young philosopher, Alexander Pfänder":

> He struck you as rather jejune and not yet a master of diction. After a few lectures in which he stuck closely to his manuscript he forced himself to speak freely and asked for indulgence for possible halts. This was something entirely new as compared with the smooth lectures of the big shots (*Bonzen*), and established at the same time an inner bond between him and us which reached far beyond the mere relation of listening. It was in tune with the deep seriousness of this incorruptible seeker for truth, who imbued every word with his subdued fervor. I always left his class deeply fortified and have never lost my gratitude to the lecturer for this early academic experience; I continued to be associated with him on the faculty of the university until his death.[8]

4. See E. Heller and F. Löw, eds., *Neue Münchener Philosophische Abhandlungen* (Leipzig, 1933).

5. "Alexander Pfänder," *Philosophy and Phenomenological Research*, II (1941), 163–65.

6. Rudolf Kindinger, ed., *Philosophenbriefe aus der wissenschaftlichen Korrespondenz von Alexius Meinong* (Graz, 1965), trans. Herbert Spiegelberg, pp. 211 f., 213 f.

7. *Grundzüge einer Metaphysik der Erkenntnis* (Berlin, 1925), p. 108.

8. Karl Alexander Müller, *Aus Gärten der Vergangenheit. Erinnerungen 1882–1914* (Stuttgart, 1958), pp. 230 f.

[III] Pfander's Place in the Phenomenological Movement

A BRIEF CHARACTERIZATION of Pfänder's relation to other and better-known members of the Phenomenological Movement seems to be in order.

As far as his connections with Husserl are concerned, the biographical section supplies the basic facts. It may be added that Husserl and Pfänder never met for more than brief visits, except for the important joint vacation in Seefeld (Tirol) in 1905. However, the ties became closer as Husserl's respect for Pfänder as the "most solid" thinker of the Munich group rose and as collaboration on the yearbook intensified. By the time that Husserl moved from Göttingen to Freiburg in 1916, he apparently felt closest to Pfänder. Thus there is almost conclusive evidence that Husserl thought of Pfänder as his most desirable successor in Freiburg until Heidegger's star began to rise. However, as Husserl moved more and more explicitly into his transcendental phenomenology and idealism, it became increasingly clear that Pfänder was not prepared to follow him. For Pfänder, along with the other members of the Munich group, stood fundamentally in the realistic tradition and tried to utilize the phenomenological approach for buttressing the realistic position. This does not mean that Pfänder was disinterested in the phenomenology of Husserl's *Ideen*. His final position, as expressed in his unpublished lectures on philosophy and phenomenology, assigned to Husserl's phenomenological reduction an important role in the framework of the phenomenological method as a preparation for an unbiased examination of the perceptual evidence which, in Pfänder's estimate, eventually supported realism. However, this was clearly no naïve realism or "ontologism," as Husserl believed. The final estrangement between the two senior members of the original phenomenological group was less a result of philosophical differences than of personal disappointments.

Thus Pfänder's position coincided with Husserl's only during the period when Husserl stressed the program of a pure logic freed of psychologism and a descriptive phenomenology of essential insights into the structures of consciousness. Nevertheless, Pfänder assimilated cautiously and selectively some of the features of Husserl's later transcendental phenomenology, such as its stress on the study of the subjective ways of viewing and on the suspension of belief (*epoché*) as an essential step in the phenomenological approach.

Pfänder's position was much closer to Scheler's. Scheler had made his first contact with Husserl in Halle in 1901. But it was only after he had transferred his lectureship from Jena to Munich in 1907 that he participated actively in the phenomenological group of which Pfänder was the leading member. While there were tremendous differences between the slow-moving and at times devastatingly critical Pfänder and the quick-minded Scheler with his uncanny speculative flair, they were comparatively close to each other in their conclusions, especially as far as their ideas about knowledge, reality, and values were concerned. At first Pfänder seems to have been severely critical of the poorly organized Scheler. But soon he recognized his genius, which he always acknowledged, even in his more speculative adventures, which he did not share.

Important philosophical differences between the two remained. While Pfänder too was concerned increasingly about the plight of modern man in an age of approaching nihilism, he did not share Scheler's social and political interests. Methodologically Pfänder was too much of the systematic logician to rival Scheler's brilliant but at times uncritical excursions and publications on the most surprising subjects. Instead, Pfänder was patiently preparing his contributions to systematic philosophy and ethics, which he presented many times in his lecture courses before formulating his final version for publication.

As far as conclusions were concerned, Pfänder's conception of the phenomenological method slowly approached Husserl's more than Scheler's. While agreeing with Scheler's realistic position, Pfänder's case differed from Scheler's stress on the experience of resistance (*Widerstand*). Pfänder's metaphysics as it gradually emerged was not based on a dichotomy as radical as Scheler's between a blind cosmic urge and a powerless spirit. Pfänder's central interest in a phenomenological and interpretive anthropological psychology led him not only to a much more systematic conception than Scheler's but to much richer content, including the development of an outspoken ego psychology and a full-fledged theory of willing and motivation. In the field of ethics Pfänder carried Scheler's distinction between value and oughtness (ideal and moral) further to the development of two equal divisions, the ethics of value and the ethics of oughtness or ideal demands. In both sections Pfänder separated systematically questions of essential structure from those of the sufficient ground for these structures, which he found in a fundamental essence (*Grundwesen*), for which there is no equivalent in Scheler. Also, Pfänder's phenomenology of religion avoided Scheler's premature theological claims, which led the latter first to a personalistic near-Catholic theism and, on the rebound, to a vague conception of a God in the making to be realized through man. Pfänder was looking cautiously for evidence of a divine ground of all being both in the outside world and within man's own being.

Any attempt to relate Pfänder to Heidegger's much more spectacular and violent use of phenomenology will have to be restricted to a mere comparison. For the personal connections between the two were at best casual. Pfänder merely watched Heidegger's emergence and rise from afar, meeting him briefly during a visit to Freiburg. But I remember from personal conversation that after the appearance of *Sein und Zeit* Pfänder predicted the failure of Heidegger's attempt to force the solution of the question of the sense of Being by the approach from *Dasein* alone. Also, he had little, if any, patience for Heidegger's style of thinking and writing, though Pfänder, whose style was always plain and avoided technical terms as far as possible, was not opposed to neologisms where they were needed for the description of overlooked phenomena. Heidegger, on his part, never made contact or showed real interest in the Munich phenomenologists. Though their phenomenological realism might have been more congenial to his enterprise than Husserl's intensifying idealism, his central concern would not have found any significant aid and comfort in their much more traditional orientation as far as general problems and solutions were concerned. Pfänder in particular made no claim that he was revolutionizing philosophy. His was a sober, painstaking effort to develop a constructive solution to the time-honored problems of philosophy by means of the new approach opened up by the phenomenological method. This did not make him a philosopher of business as usual. Behind Pfänder's attempt stood the burning concern to find a constructive answer to the challenge of Schopenhauer and Nietzsche, who had awakened him to philosophy.

[IV] The Framework of Pfänder's Philosophy

In view of the unfinished state of Pfänder's written work it would be an overstatement to present him as the author of a complete philosophical system on phenomenological grounds. Nevertheless, it can hardly be denied that he was the only one of the original members of the phenomenological movement who applied the new approach to all the major problems of philosophy, beginning with logic. Without making any explicit claims, he extended phenomenology to what is commonly called metaphysics and ontology as well as to the philosophy of nature and the theory of value.

An attempt to show the layout of Pfänder's systematic thought should ideally be based on his own "Introduction to Philosophy and Phenomenology," the lecture course which he presented sixteen times during his teaching career, modifying it each time with a view to eventual publication. It is, therefore, a particularly grave loss to phenomenology that, except for a few fragments, Pfänder was unable to complete this project. It remains to be seen how far it will be possible to construct and publish a coherent text from the skeleton notes which he worked out carefully for each lecture.

Until this problem has been solved through an edition of the original German text, all I can offer is a brief preview of the structure and the main findings of this central work as it can be anticipated from its fragmentary preparation.

To Pfänder philosophy, as distinguished from the special sciences in their essential incompleteness, was to provide terminal knowledge (*letztabschliessende Erkenntnis*) both in the sense of rounding out scientific knowledge and of determining its final significance. He divided philosophy into three major areas:

(1) "beings" (*das Seiende*) or things and our knowledge of them;

(2) values (*Werte*) and our knowledge of them;

(3) norms (*ideale Forderungen*) and our knowledge of them.

Except for the last division this grouping is clearly traditional. But it provides a framework for an unusually comprehensive application of the phenomenological approach. It is not surprising, therefore, that the actual lecture course never covered more than the first area in depth. However, as far as the philosophies of values and norms were concerned, Pfänder could refer his listeners to his lecture course on ethics, which he had offered eight times in constantly improved versions; besides, in this case he was able to complete a succinct exposition (*Kurze Darstellung*), which is practically ready for publication.

Pfänder's approach to the various problems in these areas always follows the same pattern. It begins with a critical examination of the earlier methods of sensationalist empiricism, of aprioristic rationalism, and of Kantian critical philosophy, showing in each case how far these approaches fail to give a satisfactory account of phenomena and of our knowledge of them. Only then does he introduce the phenomenological approach as he interprets it as the most adequate solution to the problems left unsolved by the other approaches.

It seems justifiable to present here a brief preview of Pfänder's main conclusions with regard to the topics he singled out for discussion and the way in which he thought phenomenology could support them. But it must be understood that such a preview merely can indicate the fruitfulness of Pfänder's approach without any pretense to making these findings sufficiently evident.

(1) Material things (*Körperdinge*) are neither complexes of sense-data, nor concepts, nor unknown *x*'s behind the sense-data, but are extended pieces of material (*Stoff*) filling space. They can be reached by a perception which utilizes sense-data as quasi-transparent appearances of these things.

(2) Space and, in a different manner, time are neither sense-data nor forms of intuition but phenomena in their own right, undefinable as such, but given directly in the perception of our own body or in that of the immediate present. On this limited basis we can reach insights into their essences which allow us to go beyond our original perception.

(3) Causality is neither a mere succession of events nor a category of the intellect but a relation in which something brings into being something else. We have primary experience of such causality through our own body.

(4) Movement is another phenomenon which can be established phenomenologically.

(5) Existence is likewise a phenomenon which is given in perception.

(6) Life and living beings mean a special range of phenomena perceivable in ourselves and in others, life being what distinguishes live and dead things and varying in different kinds of beings.

(7) The "soul" means the source of mental life given in perception of our own selves as well as in that of others.

(8) There is phenomenological evidence for "free will" in such acts as those of self-determination and in the very fact of motivation; but this is no valid reason for denying causality.

(9) However, the belief in immortality cannot be supported by phenomenological evidence.

(10) Social phenomena are *sui generis* and are given in special experiences, which can be described phenomenologically.

(11) Cultural phenomena, such as works of art, are entities in their own right, presented in experiences which permit phenomenological investigation.

(12) For religious phenomena and particularly for what we mean by the name "God," the "ground of all being," there is perceptual evidence, accessible to deepened contemplation (*Versenkung*) into the external world in its totality and into our own selves.

(13) Phenomenology of values, after clarifying the meaning of our beliefs, allows us to find in a special kind of perception such concrete value qualities as the ethical and aesthetic ones in all their variety.

(14) Ideal demands, as distinguished by a separate philosophy of norms, can be grasped in a specific perception which can be explored phenomenologically.

I repeat: it would be premature to assert that this survey amounts to a complete system of philosophy on phenomenological grounds. At best it can be considered as the scaffold for such a system. It omits the central and pervading ideas of Pfänder's philosophy, which can be found most concretely in his last work on the psyche of man, for instance, the idea that the meaning of all life is the creative unfolding (*Auszeugung*) of what each living being is at bottom (*Grundwesen*), as distinguished from what it is as an empirical fact (*empirisches Wesen*). In this sense Pfänder's philosophy of life and, more particularly, his philosophical anthropology contain the center and guiding idea of his philosophy.[9] The other parts are all related to this conception of the world as a polyphony of beings striving for harmonious unfolding.

How far Pfänder succeeded in giving enough strength to this conception, how far his system is capable of being strengthened where he could not do so himself, are questions which can only be decided by an attempt to fill out the gaps of the present sketch.

[V] PFÄNDER'S CONCEPTION OF PHENOMENOLOGY

BEFORE PRESENTING Pfänder himself by examples from his phenomenological writings, I should indicate briefly in what sense and to what extent Pfänder can be considered a phenomenologist. Actually I have already done so in the pertinent section of my historical introduction.[10] But a restatement may be in order for the benefit of those who cannot be expected to look up this discussion in its context.

Pfänder's original conception of phenomenology, a term which he adopted independently of Husserl in the title of his work, *Phe-*

9. A first idea of Pfänder's anthropology can be obtained from my article on "The Idea of a Phenomenological Anthropology and Alexander Pfänder's Psychology of Man," first published in the *Review of Existential Psychology and Psychiatry*, V (1965) and reprinted below in Appendix A, pp. 75–85, with minor changes, by permission of the Editor.

10. *The Phenomenological Movement* (2d ed.; The Hague, 1965), pp. 178–85.

nomenology of Willing, written in 1900, was that of a descriptive psychology to precede experimental work. Gradually, as the Phenomenological Movement got under way, Pfänder added the idea of insight into the "what" or the essential features and laws of the phenomena, as we can see in his study of directed sentiments ("Zur Psychology der Gesinnungen," 1913). Probably in view of Husserl's new conception of pure phenomenology as the investigation of subjectivity, the *Logik* of 1921, in admitting the difficulty of stating clearly what phenomenology is, laid special emphasis on the study of the subject's perspectives and refrained from taking a stand on the objective validity of such perspectives. Pfänder's final conception, which is much more original, is exemplified in his last unpublished works. It consists in an initial clarification of the meaning of our original beliefs about the world, mostly by determining what we mean in ordinary language in using the key terms which are later studied in philosophy, in the subsequent suspension of belief in their validity, for which Pfänder adopts Husserl's term *epoché,* and finally in the crucial test of the phenomenology of perception, which tries to establish how far our clarified meanings are supported by the findings of our perceptual experience (*Wahrnehmung*), insofar as such perception is a probing and critical one.

Thus in its final form Pfänder's phenomenology may be described as the methodical approach which, starting from the subject's meanings, by critical clarification and subsequent unbiased and thorough exploration of the phenomena tries to determine their structure in their authentic self-presence (*leibhafte Selbstgegebenheit*).

[VI] THE OUTLOOK FOR PFÄNDER IN THE ANGLO-AMERICAN WORLD

AT THIS MOMENT it would be foolhardy to make any predictions about the chances of transplanting Pfänder's philosophy into the Anglo-American world. All I feel safe in asserting is this:

Should the texts here presented arouse sufficient interest among Anglo-American readers to lead to a complete translation of some of his major works, Pfänder's philosophy could have a significant future in the English-speaking world. The best reason for such a conditional optimism seems to me to be the fact that there are new openings in this world for Pfänder's way of thinking. Recent linguistic analysis, for example, tends more and more to go beyond ordinary language to the phenomena which this language expresses. Pfänder is the phenomenologist most sympathetic to the need of an initial analysis and clarification of ordinary meanings prior to phenomenology proper.[11]

But a much more important opening may be in the area of philosophical psychology. The need for an anthropological psychology based on such concepts as self-actualization will find important support in Pfänder's phenomenological psychology of man, in which a comprehensive conception of man, free from simplistic reduction to single drives, is outlined.

[VII]   ON THE SELECTIONS

THE RATIONALE of the present selections, their potential interest to Anglo-American readers, can best be explained by describing the genesis of this volume. As stated in the beginning, its nucleus was the article on "Motives and Motivation." When the chance for further additions came, I looked primarily for pieces which would show more explicit instances of Pfänder's phenomenology.

The most obvious candidate was the *Phenomenology of Willing* of 1900. But since the inclusion of a book-length text was out of the question and since some of this work had been overtaken by "Motives and Motivation," the compromise was to introduce this text by a translation of its Introduction and to place it before "Motives and Motivation."

There might have been some point in adding the Introduction to Pfänder's first contribution to the phenomenological yearbook, "Zur Psychologie der Gesinnungen" ("Concerning the Psychology of Sentiments") of 1913 and 1916. But, illuminating though this text is, it should be published together with the main body of this study, easily Pfänder's richest phenomenological case study, which I nominate as the next candidate for a complete translation.

The third selection is the Introduction to the *Logik* of 1921. Again the inclusion of the entire book would have been impossible. But the Introduction contains one of the clearest statements of the conception of a pure logic which was announced by Husserl in the Prolegomena to the first volume of his *Logical Investigations* of 1900 and which preceded the presentation of his incipient phenomenology in the second volume. Pfänder's statement is a more fully developed version of Husserl's "pure logic," geared to its subsequent systematic development in the text. Written soon after the publication of Husserl's *Ideas*

11. For a discussion of such a convergence see my paper "Linguistic Phenomenology": John L. Austin and Alexander Pfänder, reprinted below in Appendix B, pp. 86–92.

Toward a Pure Phenomenology, it contains the most explicit statement of Pfänder's conception of phenomenology published during his lifetime.

The last selection consists of Pfänder's notes for a single lecture which he gave in Prague in 1929. The original German has been published in the Appendix to *Alexander Pfänder's Phänomenologie*, an expanded version of the section on Pfänder in *The Phenomenological Movement*. It contains the most concise formulation of Pfänder's version of phenomenology apart from the lecture course, "Introduction to Philosophy and Phenomenology." While only the latter can supply a full idea of his final conception of phenomenology, the notes for the Prague lectures give Pfänder's last articulated formulation of it. This may justify its publication in the present volume.

In translating Pfänder's German, which, compared with that of other phenomenologists, is unusually plain, though not always elegant, I have striven for the least unhappy medium between faithfulness and readability. Generally, I have leaned toward faithfulness, as shown by my often adding the German word after the English expression whenever I did not find a clear and adequate equivalent for it. But in the interest of better readability I cut down drastically on Pfänder's German custom of excessive italicizing, retaining it chiefly in places where without the added stress one would misread the sentence.

HERBERT SPIEGELBERG

Washington University
St. Louis
February 1967

Phenomenology of Willing
and Motivation

1 / Introduction to the *Phenomenology* of *Willing*

PFÄNDER'S *Phenomenology of Willing*, of which I translated merely the Introduction, was first published in 1900 by Johann Ambrosius Barth in Leipzig; a second unchanged edition appeared in 1930, combined with "Motive und Motivation"; and a third edition, also unchanged, was included in the *Gesammelte Schriften* in 1963. Such sustained interest through three generations is in itself a testimony to the continuing value of this study.

The little book was not Pfänder's first publication on the subject. It was preceded by his Munich dissertation, in which he had subjected to a critical examination the major theories of willing of Hugo Münsterberg, William James, Oswald Külpe, Théodule Ribot, and Wilhelm Wundt, and by reviews of two other works on the will. The main point of these studies was to show that willing can never be reduced to representations (*Vorstellungen*) or sensations (*Empfindungen*). The *Phänomenologie des Wollens* was Pfänder's first independent attempt to present a positive account of willing.

The main body of the book consists of two sections, one on the consciousness of willing in the general sense of the consciousness of striving, the other on the consciousness of willing in the narrower sense. In the first section, which amounts to almost two-thirds of the text, striving, which includes wishing, hoping, longing, desiring, fearing, and despising, is explored. Among its essential characteristics we find the act of intending (*Meinen*) of something absent which is considered to be a goal; its relation to pleasure and displeasure is investigated, and the feeling of a pressing or tending toward (and a corresponding pressing or tending against something in counterstriving) is described.

What distinguishes willing in the narrower sense from striving is, first of all, the belief that what is striven for can be brought about by one's own doing and, secondly, that the range of this striving extends to the conditions of its realization, including one's own doing. But what converts such striving into willing in the proper sense is that the ego sides spontaneously with such striving. In the course of this investigation, such concepts as end, means, choice, decision, and motive are discussed.

It may not be inappropriate to consider the relation of such a "phenomenology" of the will to the recent attack on the "myth of volition" by Gilbert Ryle.[1] First I want to point out that the title of Pfänder's book is not *Phenomenology of the Will* (*Wille*) but *Phenomenology of Willing* (*Wollen*). In other words, Pfänder is concerned not with any more or less hypothetical faculty of the psyche in the sense of metaphysical psychology, but with concrete acts of willing. Now, it is true that Ryle, at least on the face of it, denies even acts of volition as separate from one's actual doing, although he does admit that we might do things voluntarily or involuntarily. Of course his evidence for such a denial is at best linguistic, based on the observation of concrete ordinary language. It leads Ryle to assert that "the doctrine of volitions is a casual hypothesis" (p. 67). It is precisely this kind of a metatheory which a phenomenology in Pfänder's style can put to the test. Such a phenomenological test is even more pertinent, since Pfänder insists from the very start on basing his study on the ordinary usage of the word "willing"; of course, this means the ordinary German usage, which might be more favorable to his case than English, but, in view of the English use of the word "will" even in the future tense of the verb, it hardly is.

Other features of the Introduction worth underlining are: the parallel of Brentano-Husserl's "intentionality" in the essential reference of willing to something object-like that is willed; its connection with thinking; the whole emphasis on the subjective approach as indispensable in a study of willing, rather than on what is merely accidental to it. This is indeed more than mere description of the particular. At least by implication, here are the beginnings of an eidetic phenomenology of the essential structure of willing.—H.S.

ACCORDING TO A DIVISION which has become current since Kant's time, willing, together with thinking and feeling, completes the series of psychic events. Without denying that there is a factual justification for the distinction of these three species of psychic events, one still has to challenge this division if it involves the assumption that these three species cover the range of psychology and that there are no psychic events besides them. Psychology as the science of psychic events deals not only with thinking, feeling, and willing, but also, for example, with perceptions and representations (*Vorstellungen*). True, one can extend the concept of thinking so far that one includes in it perceptions and representations. But even then, this division, if meant as a division of the field of psychology, is still defective in several regards. To begin with, the division is not clean-cut. For, as will appear more clearly later, there is no willing in which thinking and feeling do not constitute essential ingredients. Likewise, in thinking, feeling plays an essential part in the form of logical feelings, and at least part of thinking is a species of willing, namely a striving for certainty or truth.

This intimate interpenetration of thinking, feeling, and willing

1. *The Concept of Mind* (London, 1949), chap. III ("The Will").

makes it impossible to subject one of these types to psychological analysis all by itself. Accordingly, an analysis of willing cannot avoid a consideration of thinking and feeling insofar as they are ingredients of willing.

Another defect of the above division is that the words "thinking," "feeling," and "willing" stress exclusively the subjective side of these psychic processes as behaviors of an ego. But thinking, feeling, and willing are completely suspended in mid-air as empty possibilities if one detaches them from the material to which they refer. Sensations and representations, in the sense of contents of sensations and representations or units of sensations and representations as well as their spatial and temporal relations, form the material, as it were, on which thinking and willing operate and to which feelings refer. This material, this "object-like" referent (*Gegenständliches*) of consciousness, is also part of the psychic reality, hence also part of the domain of psychology, and therefore must not be excluded by the preceding division.

True, one asserts again and again that everything "object-like" is to be excluded from psychology. It is stated that the subject matter of psychology is not the contents of sensations, representations, and the like, but rather sensing, representing, etc.; in short, that psychology is the science of the "inner" or psychic "states" (*Zustände*) and not of the contents (*Inhalte*) of consciousness. But even a simple look at today's psychology shows that psychology does not deal solely with such "states." There is no psychology of mere states, and there cannot be one. The reason for the opposite contention is not the facts but the necessity of cutting off the domain of psychology from that of natural science. It is thought that one can establish such a sharp demarcation only by assigning to psychology the states, to the physical sciences the contents.

On the other hand, the assertion that for psychology there are only "object-like" contents is equally lopsided. People have tried to restrict psychology, and specifically the psychology of willing, to the consideration of sensations and representations; it has been believed that psychology, if it wants to fulfill its proper task, must admit only sensations or representations, or even sensations alone, as ultimate elements of all psychic events. Such assertions usually are based not on facts, but on general considerations and unrelated motives such as the narrowing look toward a "mechanical" or "physiological" explanation of psychic data, or the bias for what, in the sensations and representations, is seemingly tangible and resistant to the grip, and the aversion to everything which does not appear to be visible (*anschaulich*) but is nebulous and slips away between our fingers.

Here too the mere consideration of the psychological investigations shows that there is no such thing as a science of psychic life which would operate merely with sensations and representations and that wherever such a thing seems to exist, the concepts which are allegedly used for the designation of complexes of sensations and representations actually mean more than mere sensations and representations; otherwise, such descriptions of the psychic facts would simply not apply. True, there are also such "psychological" investigations as, in order to stick consistently to their general view, do not shrink from doing violence to the facts by declaring arbitrarily that such and such a complex of sensations or representations constitute the entire psychic fact to be analyzed. Especially in the case of willing, such dictates (*Machtsprüche*) are not infrequent.

Now in the following text considerations of other more general problems will not determine how willing is to be characterized, how physical phenomena can be distinguished from psychic ones, or what kind of solution the problem of willing must have if it is to admit of a physiological interpretation or satisfy subjective needs for visualization (*Anschaulichkeit*) and tangibility. Hence, we shall at the outset include willing neither among the "states" or "acts" nor among the "contents," in the sense of object-like contents such as sensations and representations, but first of all we shall try to determine willing in its actual peculiarity.

To be sure, if one practiced respect (*Pietät*) toward the psychic facts, it would appear that both "states" and "contents" are part of willing. It would follow from this that psychology, in whose domain willing undeniably belongs, is to deal with "states" or "acts" and "contents." However, controversies over such questions easily degenerate into verbal arguments, since the concepts of "state" or "act" and "content" often are not used in the same unambiguous sense. Hence, I shall let these questions rest.

Furthermore, let it be left completely undecided whether willing occurs only in man or also among animals, plants, or in the inorganic world. It does seem certain that there is no sufficient reason for assuming willing in the world of plants or inorganic matter. But a final decision about this can only be made once it is established what willing really is. And this investigation can be carried out directly only for *human* willing. Hence, only human willing is to be the theme of this investigation.

Whether or not human willing is the basic function of human psychic life, whether or not all psychic processes are nothing but modes of expressing the will, whether or not all psychic events are fundamentally cases of willing—all such general assertions must at first be suspended. For an investigation of human willing must always start from the ordinary usage of the verbal noun "willing." And this usage includes the assumption not that every conceivable psychic event is a willing, but rather that only specifically qualified psychic facts deserve the name of "willing." Of course, starting from this assumption does not imply uncritical belief in its correctness. Rather, establishing the characteristic quality of those psychic facts which are designated specifically as willing decides at the same time the question whether or not it is justified to contrast willing as a peculiar fact with other psychic events.

We know of psychic facts only through the phenomena of *consciousness (Bewusstseinserscheinungen)*. If, therefore, willing is to be a special psychic fact, there must be phenomena of consciousness which in their peculiarity constitute precisely what is ultimately meant by "willing." So the first need is the exploration and analysis of these facts of consciousness, of conscious willing or the consciousness of willing, if the fact of willing is to be known. Of course by "consciousness of willing" we are to understand not the knowledge of the fact that a person is willing something, but simply that fact of consciousness which exists when someone wills something, regardless of whether he states or records at the same time that he wills it right now.

Now one can consider as the conscious fact of willing the entire psychic process which begins with a deliberation of will or choice and with the solution of more or less difficult questions and conflicts, which then becomes the fact of willing proper by the decision or resolution, and which finally, with the continued action and direction of willing, leads to the realization of what is willed, i.e., to the choice of the concrete means and the successive realization of the specific means. To analyze the entire process of willing, therefore, would require a detailed analysis of these stages.

However, we shall learn what constitutes willing as a conscious experience only through analysis of the fact which begins with the decision or resolution. The total process is called willing only because it contains, besides the preparatory factors and consequences, this very fact of willing. The explicit deliberation, the choice and the decision of will, as well as the immediate consequence of the realization, may be missing, and yet all of the constitutive elements of the consciousness of willing can be there, provided that the stage of the total process is present which begins with the decision.

The main subject for an analysis of the consciousness of willing is, therefore, that intermediate stage which may first be designated as a state of volitional inner-directedness toward something. So in what follows we shall be less occupied with deliberation and choice, let alone with the realization of what is willed, than with the more detailed analysis of that state of affairs which lies between them. Anyhow, the psychic event which precedes or follows certain facts of consciousness cannot serve directly as their definition but can only provide pointers for their more precise determination.

This determination of the theme of the investigation settles at the same time the only possible method of investigation. For if it is necessary for the clarification of the facts of willing to analyze the consciousness of willing, only the purely psychological way can lead to it, that is, the method which investigates the conscious facts of willing itself. This so-called "subjective" method does not necessarily consist in a direct observation of what is immediately experienced; for this is mostly, and especially in the case of willing, impossible. Rather the "subjective" method starts by necessity from the fixation of the immediate or more remote images in memory. Hence, this "introspective" method or method of "inner observation," as it has been erroneously named, is actually not "introspective" but is mostly "retrospective." Even if it includes defects and dangers, it is after all the only possible method.

True, much is said now about so-called "objective methods," and it is thought that, since elsewhere only the "objective" has significance for science, these objective methods are to be recommended as the only scientific ones. However, in this case the "objective" does not have the same weight which it has elsewhere, since here it means something quite different. These "objective" methods try to determine and know psychic events by way of observation of the "external" bodily processes which other people can observe. Now psychic processes are indeed in close connection with various other processes in the human body and thus also with processes in the so-called external world. And it is not only of interest, but it is even a necessary scientific task to investigate these relations and to recognize them and their laws. But by mere inspection and observation of bodily processes one does not obtain insight into the psychic processes which are related to them. If one wants to describe what property or change of a psychic process corresponds to an observed property or change of a bodily process, one must have a regular relation between psychic and bodily processes as a guideline, and, besides, one must know the area and the regular changes in this field to which one is led by that guideline. All so-called objective psychological methods presuppose the application of the so-called subjective method. The objective method, therefore, can be only an auxiliary method for psychology but cannot constitute *the* psychological method.

Even the psychological investigation of willing will not be able to reach its goal by the so-called objective methods alone. Willing must have been cleared up in its essence, to some degree, before one can undertake to correlate with it certain physiological or physical processes and to infer backward from the quality of the latter to that of willing. After all, one can never determine immediately from the looks of physiological and physical processes whether they are conditioned by willing or something else, or whether psychic processes definitely correspond to them at all.

Thus it becomes manifest that wherever one is not clear about this relation but rather thinks one can offer a "physiological" or so-called "psycho-physical" theory of willing without first making a thorough psychological analysis of the facts of consciousness, one does not speak of willing at all. Instead, one is really speaking of all sorts of other things, or else one uses, uncritically and without knowing what one is doing, the spontaneously arising psychology of daily life as a guide to completely hypothetical constructions of physiological processes. One presupposes as known what one would like to know and wraps up the already known in new expressions; one merely illustrates the popular psychology of willing by metaphors, images, pictures of external processes—hence the plausibility and the intellectually soporific influence of such theories.

By this I do not mean to say that popular psychology has no right to be considered. On the contrary, greater attention to it than usual would be highly desirable. For the facts of consciousness are accessible to everyone's eyes; there are few facts of psychology which have not been experienced at some time by every normal adult. There is nothing new to be discovered here. It can be anticipated, therefore, that popular psychology contains many a correct observation. But it is not only possible, it is even necessary that it serve as the point of departure for scientific psychology, considering the fact that there is no other point of departure for the adult person. Only the uncritical and unscientific acceptance of it is not to be recommended. Rather, the descriptions and explanations which popular psychology, embodied in language and linguistic usage, offers for the psychic facts must be checked against them and possibly subjected to correction. This means that in all cases psychology must proceed to the analysis of the facts of consciousness themselves.

Thus the psychology of willing has to abide by the conscious data of willing itself. Specifically, it is impossible to determine willing by bodily movements whose execution is frequently a means to achieving the intended end and to define willing, for example, simply as the "cause of bodily movements." For there are innumerable bodily movements which do not have any demonstrable psychic cause at all. But even the definition of willing as "the *psychic* cause of bodily movements" makes no sense. For the so-called expressive movements also have a psychic cause, but this cause is precisely *not* a willing. On the other hand, although willing may frequently be the cause of bodily movements, there are also various kinds of willing which are directed toward things other than bodily movements, e.g., voluntary attentiveness, reflecting, thinking, etc. Besides, this supposed definition does not define willing itself; from it we do not learn what is the nature of the conscious data of willing.

To analyze a fact of consciousness means to divide it into its parts or elements and specifically into both its separable parts and those which are distinguishable only *in abstracto*. It also means to dissolve possible products of fusion and to raise into consciousness elements which are frequently left in the unconscious. In short, the first and foremost task of psychology is fulfilled by establishing the regularity (*Gesetzmässigkeit*) of the being or the nature of the psychic facts. But in the end psychology must not be satisfied with carrying out this first assignment. Rather, its final task lies in the *explanation* of psychic happenings, in the tracing of causal relations between the single elements of the conscious facts, if necessary by the complementary assumption of underlying processes. General laws of psychic happenings have to be sought out from which the single concrete conscious experiences can be explained. But this task presupposes the accomplishment of the former one. The obtaining of laws of psychic happening must start from the investigation of the immediate facts of consciousness. And if one believes he has found laws among certain facts, the question arises whether they are sufficient for explaining other psychic facts. But in that case the factual complexes to be explained must be presented with sufficient precision and completeness.

Experience impresses on us the need for this procedure by showing that almost all controversies in psychology finally go back to the question of the nature of certain conscious facts. Basically the explanation of psychological facts would be a relatively simple task if only what is to be explained were definitely established in its nature. But conscious phenomena are made of not very solid and easily perishable material, as it were. They, therefore, prove to have very little resistance, if an "intellect" making deductions from ready-made laws assails them in order to put them into a theoretical strait jacket. The theoretical explanation obtained is then seemingly correct. The "intellect" appears to have reached its goal of simplification and flexible explanation but has at the same time concealed the abundance of psychic life by the breastplate of elegant logical constructions. In that case satisfaction at the theoretical achievement easily prevents awareness of the poverty of the picture from becoming apparent. Once, however, the conscious phenomena are completely and respectfully recorded, they possess more resistance to the attempt to press them into a rigid theoretical dress by force and thereby are more likely to obtain a garment which snugly fits their rich development.

For the psychology of willing, too, the real and final task is to find causal relations, to explain willing and to formulate laws of willing. But here too the facts themselves, hence in the first place the consciousness of willing, have to be investigated and established before the explanation can be started.

In what follows, what is to be attempted is exclusively the analysis of the conscious facts of willing in the above-mentioned sense but not an explanation of the processes of willing. The danger of onesidedness usually attached to psychological investigations of a limited aspect of psychic happenings is thereby automatically eliminated. For, as noted before, willing is closely intertwined with representations and feelings, or rather it contains them. A precise analysis of the facts of willing, therefore, cannot be offered without considering ideas and feelings. Hence, in what follows a good deal will have to be said about representations and feelings.

A comprehensive, and in all respects exhaustive, treatment of the problem of willing would have as its final result an almost complete psychology, a psychology, however, in which the problem of willing would stand in the forefront of interest.

2 / Motives and Motivation

THE RELEVANCE of Pfänder's essay on "Motive und Motivation" for Anglo-American readers may be far from obvious. My own discussion of Pfänder as one of the early but neglected phenomenologists in my historical introduction to the Phenomenological Movement [1] does not supply justification for this particular choice. A more timely reason could be the fact that Paul Ricoeur, after mentioning this essay repeatedly in his *Philosophie de la volonté*,[2] referred to it specifically during his recent lectures in the United States. Also, Ludwig Binswanger wrote in 1942: "Even today, the best that has been written about motivation is Pfänder's phenomenological study 'Motive und Motivation'." [3]

However, the best reason for making Pfänder's essay accessible in English at this time is its dovetailing with R. S. Peters' brilliant study *The Concept of Motivation*.[4] Before reading it, I felt uneasy about the relevance of Pfänder's discussion of motivation to the Anglo-American world. I no longer do. Peters' "missionary enterprise" (p. 148) of restoring the terms "motive" and "motivation" to their rightful places in ordinary language and his critique of the artificiality of their scientific uses are also the best possible defense for Pfänder, who takes these ordinary uses for granted, at least in the present essay. Now all that Peters claims for his monograph is that "like an underground movement, it delivers thrusts at the established order in psychology from within, but never comes above ground to make any positive suggestions" (p. 153 f.); and he adds that "different and logically appropriate theories should be developed to answer different sorts of questions, rather than all-inclusive theories to answer all of them" (*ibid.*). This is precisely what Pfänder undertakes by way of positive phenomenological descriptions of what the terms "motive" and "motivation" stand for in ordinary usage. Peters' chapter on "Motives and Motivation," although written more than four decades later, can serve as a fitting prolegomena for Pfänder's pioneering study, not only for today's philosophers, but for all those who have accepted the usual psychological terminology.

1. *The Phenomenological Movement* (2d ed.; The Hague, 1965), chap. IV.
2. See the seven references listed in the English translation of this work, *Freedom and Nature*, trans. Erazím V. Kohák (Evanston, Ill., 1966).
3. *Grundforman und Erkenntnis menschlichen Daseins* (2d ed.; Zurich, 1953), p. 688.
4. *The Concept of Motivation* (London, 1958).

[12]

The original text appeared in the *Münchener Philosophische Abhandlungen*, a *Festschrift* prepared in 1911 for Theodor Lipps on his sixtieth birthday by his former students, for whom Pfänder acted as the main editor. It is not inconceivable that Pfänder avoided explicit reference to phenomenology in his essay out of consideration for Lipps, who was smarting under the defection of most of his own students to Husserl's new movement. When a second edition of Pfänder's *Phänomenologie des Wollens* appeared in 1930, he added this essay as "a continuation and partial correction." Yet it clearly does not presuppose a knowledge of the earlier book for adequate understanding.

The place of this essay in the sequence of Pfänder's publications is after his *Einführung in die Psychologie* of 1904 and before his "Zur Psychologie der Gesinnungen" of 1913 and 1916, his first contribution to Husserl's *Jahrbuch für Philosophie und phänomenologische Forschung*, of which Pfänder was one of the original co-editors. The essay belongs, therefore, in the period in Pfänder's development during which he was particularly interested in a phenomenological psychology which would widen and deepen the exploration of psychic phenomena and determine their essential nature. However, "Motive und Motivation" points beyond this more limited objective to his ultimate concern for an interpretive psychology (*verstehende Psychologie*), as developed in his final work *Die Seele des Menschen*. For an understanding of motivation is basic for such a comprehensive interpretation of the human psyche.

Pfänder's use of the term "psychology of motivation" is far different from its usual meaning, particularly in Anglo-American psychology. For Pfänder's conception of motive is deliberately much narrower than that of most other studies of motivation. Thus it differs from the usual American conception of motive as an "explanation of why a person behaves as he does." [5] It differs even from the current German usage, in which "motive" is described as the "ensemble of incentives." [6] In fact, in the *Phänomenologie des Wollens*, Pfänder himself had defined "motive" as the "striving for the final goal," [7] though even then he did distinguish it from mere unconscious causes of willing. At this point, he apparently made one of those corrections of the earlier work to which he alludes in the introduction to "Motive und Motivation." This is one of those characteristic phenomenological redefinitions which can and must result from a more careful investigation of the phenomena.

Pfänder's restricted sense of the term "motive" is, however, in line with the French sense of *motive* as the more reflexive determinant of action, compared with *mobile* as the more passionate one, a distinction which goes back to Pierre Janet (see LaLande, *Vocabulaire technique et critique de la philosophie* under *mobile*, an equivalent of the German *Triebfeder*).[8]

5. David C. McClellan, "Motivation," *Encyclopaedia Britannica* (Chicago, 1965), XV, 919–24.

6. *Antriebe*. Cf. Wilhelm Hehlmann, "Motiv," *Wörtenbuch der Psychologie* (Stuttgart, 1959), p. 224.

7. *Phänomenologie des Wollens* (1st ed.; Leipzig, 1900), p. 100; 3rd ed. (Munich, 1963), p. 92.

8. Incidentally, this is one of the cases where the translation of Jean-Paul Sartre's *L'Être et le néant* by Hazel Barnes proves to be unhappily misleading by rendering the French *mobile* by the English "motive" and the French *motive* by the English "cause" (*Being and Nothingness* [New York, 1948], pp. 436 ff.),

Apart from this major problem of interpretation, I have run into a number of more specific quandaries in the rendering of such terms as *geistig*. The solutions of the more important ones are explained in footnotes underneath the text where these expressions first occur.[9]

In conclusion I would like to point out the relation of Pfänder's conception of motivation to the one developed by another phenomenologist, Alfred Schütz. In his theory of social action, Schütz distinguished between two types of motives, the "in-order-to motive" and the "because-of motive," one dealing with the project in the future, as pursued by the action, the other with the circumstances in the past which account for the action.[10] In making this distinction, Schütz, who was aware and highly appreciative of Pfänder's essay, in following Max Weber seems to introduce a kind of motivation not discussed by Pfänder, who discusses only "because-of motives" and actually only "subjective" because-of motives. For Pfänder "in-order-to" motives would presumably figure only as goals of acts of willing. However, Schütz was certainly right in thinking that in ordinary language we refer to such goals as motives, too. In this case, the important task would be to determine whether and how far Pfänder's analysis of the "because-of motives" also applies to the "in-order-to motives" and, if not, what modifications would have to be made to include them.—H. S.

INTRODUCTION

WITHOUT NOTICING IT, people connect very different meanings with the word "motive," which plays such an important role in psychology and ethics. The facts to which these meanings point have been grasped only remotely and according to their general similarities, but their essential differences, which on closer inspection reveal themselves distinctly, have been completely overlooked. The result is a confusion and mixture of thought with a homonymic terminology for very different things. Thus the discussion of many controversial questions, for instance the question of free will and the question of whether only actions determined by a sense of duty or also those determined by inclination can be moral, has been reduced to a seemingly hopeless confusion which enmeshes and threatens to smother completely every beginning student.

In the following pages a comprehensive study of the facts and their essential nature, as accurate a study as possible, will show that the

---

although Sartre himself uses the French *cause* in the universal sense *pas de phénomène sans cause*. Sartre's *motive*, depending as it does on the will which supports itself by the motive (since consciousness confers the meaning of *motive* or *mobile* in the context of its projects) comes very close to Pfänder's conception.

9. The German text for this translation is that of the third edition, *Phänomenologie des Wollens* (Munich, 1963), pp. 125–56.

10. See *Collected Papers*, II (The Hague, 1962), pp. 21 f., 69 ff.; also more fully in *Der Sinnhafte Aufbau der sozialen Welt* (2d ed.; Vienna, 1960), pp. 57, 93 ff.

ground of will must be distinguished from its *cause* just as strictly as the ground of knowledge is set apart from its cause; that the *motivation* of willing is completely different from the *causation* of willing; and hence that the two must be kept well apart in our thinking. It is advisable to reserve the word "motive" exclusively for the motivation of willing and to use other words for whatever stands in some other relation to willing. However, I shall not show here what an extraordinary significance the clarification of this point can have for psychology and ethics. Only briefly will I indicate at the end that the insights thus obtained can also open a vista upon a new discipline analogous to logic, namely, a theory of the objects of will (*voluntaria*) and of their sufficient grounds. In passing, I should like to point out that the present studies contain a continuation and a partial correction of what I have written on the topic in my *Phenomenology of Willing* (1900).

I owe much stimulation and the incentive for a renewed exploration of the motivation of the will to Andreas Thomsen's detailed investigations into the concept of the criminal motive.[11] My present findings do not agree with his. Unfortunately, limitations of space do not permit me to discuss his investigations as thoroughly as they deserve.

The area of facts to which one must turn in order to receive the desired elucidation about motives as grounds of will is the field of willing. In this field all processes which end up in the purely inner act of willing (*Willensakt*), i.e., the act of volitional proposing, can be distinguished from those which are part of the volitional execution of what is willed and which in their entirety are to be designated here as actions of willing (*Willenshandlungen*). The distinction between the act of willing and the action of willing is possible even in those cases in which the action of willing follows immediately, without hesitation, upon the act of willing. The initiating impulses (*Willensimpulse*) which occur in the action of willing are, to be sure, in a certain sense also acts of willing, but they are nevertheless different from the act of volitional proposing, to which they are at the same time subordinated. Aiming at the intent of the will (*Vorsatz*), kept firmly and persistently in mind and using it as support, the ego carries out its initiating impulses one after another in succession. Now there are grounds for the act of willing as well as for the initiating impulses of willing and the action of willing. In the following essay, however, this investigation is to be limited to the grounds of the *act of willing*. To be sure, the question whether an act of willing, that is, real willing, can take place without an action of willing following it immediately or following it at all must be answered in the affirmative, as has been demonstrated

11. *Untersuchungen über den Begriff des Verbrechensmotifs* (Munich, 1902).

sufficiently in the psychological literature. In cases where the action of willing does not follow, neither the facts nor language justify calling the act of will a mere wishing, since wishing differs essentially from willing not by the lack of the following action, but by completely different factors. Yet however this may be, first the act of willing and its motivation must be discussed separately. The results thus obtained make it easy to formulate the solution of the corresponding questions regarding the motivation of the *action* of willing and of the initiating *impulses,* while conversely, if one tries to treat these latter questions first, one is of necessity taken back to the question of the motivation of the *act* of willing.

Now the nature of the motivation of willing cannot be cleared up without previous knowledge of and steady attention to the special nature of the act of willing. To this end the investigation will first go into the psychological facts of striving, to which the act of willing will then be contrasted and characterized in its peculiar nature. Next, the relations of the act of willing to what "precedes" it, in different senses of this word, will be explored, and the specific motivational relation will be isolated and determined in its essence.

[I] THE FIELD OF STRIVINGS

1. General Analysis of the Case of Striving

CERTAIN OBJECTS, or states of affairs, or events which are felt, perceived, remembered, represented, or merely thought by a human individual, arouse in him certain strivings or counterstrivings. By no means always, but only extremely rarely are these strivings directed toward or against feelings of pleasure or displeasure. There is a striving to feel or sensuously perceive something; to notice or to apperceive something; to visualize something; to recognize, to learn to know, to believe, to affirm, to infer, to support, to prove, to explain something; there is likewise a striving to get oneself into certain moods, to develop, diminish, or prolong them. Similar strivings are directed toward analogous goals in feelings of all sorts and in directed sentiments (*Gesinnungen*). And finally striving can also be directed toward the realization or non-realization of external objects, states of affairs, and events.

In a given case, let there be an object in our consciousness which arouses a striving; let an orange be perceived and arouse a striving to eat it. Then what is before us as a knowable fact is first of all a certain consciousness of an object. This consciousness contains at least a certain relation in which at first an ego as subject simply confronts an object *qua object*. But from this ego as a center different kinds of centrifugal "movements" can go toward the confronting object. One of these centrifugal "movements" is the act of *attending*, or figuratively speaking, the centrifugal radiating of the light of consciousness toward the object, which is *different* from *apperceiving*, from mentally reaching out, seizing, selecting, abstracting, separating, and collecting. Under certain circumstances attending and apperceiving are joined by *questioning* and *pointing*—likewise centrifugally directed but different—and in addition finally by *asserting*, the thought-forming mental *projecting*, and *setting apart*.

Now if the object toward which the ego in its object-consciousness is somehow turned centrifugally arouses a striving in the ego, such arousing is experienced as a centripetal ignition, a lighting of an *impelling* striving, which issues from the object which confronts us—a process which is obscure in its course and bursts into a bright flame only in a special part of the ego. Put differently, the whole situation has more the character of an attraction (or repulsion), which issues from the object, moves centripetally toward the ego, attacks it at a certain point, and moves back centrifugally.

Besides the centrifugal object-consciousness and the centripetal arousing, the fact of striving contains also striving itself as a new and different kind of centrifugal aiming or "movement." Striving always has a centrifugal direction, but in itself it is blind; it is not itself a consciousness of a certain goal, nor does it necessarily contain such a consciousness. What is however constitutive for each striving is an inner polar duality, i.e., in it a centrifugal current is fused with an opposite inner resistance to form a genuine unit with a definite character of tension.[12]

Besides this basic duality, striving shows yet another distinctive duality; it is either a striving *toward* something or a counterstriving *against* something. In the former (striving toward) the current which constitutes the striving aims at the reduction of the non-real (*ideell*) distance between ego and object. In the latter (striving against), however, it aims at widening of this distance. And the resistance which co-constitutes the striving is, in the case of striving toward, directed [likewise] toward an enlargement of the distance.

Now in the total situation of striving those three directions or "movements" which go back and forth between ego and object stand to each other in certain relations. The centrifugal object-consciousness establishes a contact between object and ego, which then makes it

12. Cf. Theodor Lipps, *Leitfaden der Psychologie* (3rd ed.; Leipzig, 1909), p. 260.

possible for the object to attack the ego directly and to arouse a striving in it. Once the contact is established, the origin of this striving in the ego is an occurrence which takes place without the ego's cooperation, an occurrence which is phenomenally caused or possibly merely aroused by the confronting object. The centrifugal direction of the object-consciousness, therefore, is followed in the object, as a turning point (*Knickpunkt*), by the centripetal direction of this arousal, which then induces in the ego, as a turning point, the rise of a centrifugal striving. If the content or the kind of object-consciousness changes, the strivings aroused or caused in the ego keep on changing.

2. Phenomenal Source, Phenomenal Cause, and Real Cause of Striving

IN THESE STRIVINGS one must distinguish (1) the phenomenal source of the striving, (2) the phenomenal cause of the striving, and (3) the real cause of the striving. If, for instance, a heard noise arouses a striving to look toward a certain spot in the surrounding space, the phenomenal *source* of this striving is the ego or a certain state of feeling of the ego: a feeling of lack, of insufficiency, or of displeasure. However, the *phenomenal cause* of this striving is the heard noise by which this striving is aroused. And the *real cause* of this striving is a voluminous complex of psycho-physical conditions in the psycho-physical individual and his present physical environment. Neither the source, nor the phenomenal cause, nor the real cause, nor even an element of the real cause of striving is, as such, what is later to be called a motive. Even when the phenomenal source of striving is itself another striving, this relation of the experienced issuance of the one striving out of another cannot be considered as a relation of motivation in the sense still to be determined.

3. Eccentric and Central Strivings

THE STRIVINGS AND COUNTERSTRIVINGS originating in the ego do not always have the same location in it. For this ego has a characteristic structure: the ego-center (*Ich-Zentrum*), or the ego-core, is surrounded by an ego-body (*Ich-Leib*). And the strivings can arise in the ego, but outside the ego-center in the ego-body, and hence, in this sense, can be experienced as eccentric strivings. Probably most strivings and counterstrivings in the adult human being have at first this eccentric location, whose eccentricity, by the way, may have different degrees.

Now, like all strivings, these eccentric strivings have by themselves a centrifugal direction pointing away from the ego. But at the same time they have a tendency to shift from their eccentric location into a central one, or to seize the ego-center and pull it inside. This tendency can then more or less quickly reach its goal; the central ego can be quickly seized and held down without its will, now by this, now by that striving as it emerges eccentrically. Finally, from the very start, the central ego can, without a will and naïvely, be within the strivings as they arise; hence, these strivings can be in this sense original and central. In all these possible cases, any willing—about which we shall not speak till later—must be kept out. The experienced relation of the eccentric strivings to the ego-center is a phenomenal causing, not yet by any means a motivation. The fact that the ego-center is drawn into these strivings is by itself no act of willing. The central striving which usurps the ego is, therefore, not yet a willing. And the original and central striving mentioned above must be carefully distinguished from a will-like striving, which is original and central in a completely different sense.

The consideration of the ego-center mentioned here shows that it is by no means identical with the momentarily "strongest" or with the "lasting and constant" strivings; in fact, this identity, which has been asserted now and then, is impossible. For the ego is always the subject of the strivings, never the striving itself, and still less a sum of the strivings.

4. Plurality of Simultaneous Strivings

SUPPOSE A PLURALITY of mutually conflicting strivings occurs simultaneously in the ego, and, after a shorter or longer period, one of the strivings "conquers" the opposing ones—the "conquering" one is not only stronger but is the only one to seize the ego-center and pull it into itself—and leads, as the usurping and central striving, to the realization of what is striven for. Suppose, for instance, the striving aroused by a noise to look at a certain spot in surrounding space leads, in spite of the counterstriving against the expected pains in the eye, to actual looking. All this in itself is not yet any kind of willing and can thus in principle occur in man without any true act of willing. To be sure, with regard to the "conquering" striving, one can inquire into its phenomenal source or its phenomenal and its actual cause and also into the cause of its victory. But the very thing which later is to be designated as motive, namely, the ground of willing, is different from all these, and here it is not yet present at all. If the striving "conquers" the other opposing strivings in its struggle for the ego-center, for instance, that counterstriving against pains in the eye, this process is essentially different from the process in which the ego lets itself be induced to a certain willing by a motive. In the former case, the ego-center is simply the apple of discord which, even though it is perhaps a spectator, nevertheless, without his will becomes the prey of the stronger contender. In the second case, however, that lack of willing intervenes as something completely new and stands in relation both to its motive and to the motive-obeying behavior of the ego in phenomenologically quite different relations from those in which the ego-center stands to that stronger striving and its "victory." Keeping in mind the characteristic mechanisms of the life of striving which has been briefly described here, we now turn to the act of willing.

[II] THE ESSENTIAL NATURE OF THE ACT OF WILLING

COMPARED WITH MERE STRIVINGS and counterstrivings, with the "victory of the strongest striving" and its usurping of the ego, the act of willing is something completely new. First it will be distinguished from other facts, and then it will be characterized according to its special nature. This nature is connected with the possibility of a special type of relation which it can have toward certain conscious facts, a relation which is to be designated as a relation of motivation.

1. Distinction of the Act of Willing from Other Facts

THE ACT OF WILLING differs first of all, just as striving does, from mere object-consciousness, from paying attention, from apperceiving, from the questioning and pointing which refers to something (*Hinzielen*). It is, therefore, no mere act of attention, no mere act of apperception, and no mere foresight of a psychic effect. For in a given case all this may be present without the performance of any act of willing.

The act of willing differs from striving, too. It differs from eccentric striving by the fact that it is always central, which is to say that it is performed by the ego-center itself. Besides, it differs from the original and central striving mentioned above by the fact that here the ego-center is not only the subject and origin but also the original performer of the act. Phenomenally, the act of willing appears precisely *not* as an occurrence caused by a different agent but as an initial act of the ego-center itself.

Although the act of willing agrees with striving, inasmuch as it has centrifugal direction, it is, nevertheless, in complete contrast with striving, not blind per se but containing in its essence a consciousness of what is willed. True, the performance of the act of willing is a striving action, in which the centrifugal current contained in the constituting polarity [of striving and counterstriving] overcomes its inner inhibition by its own force. The performance, therefore, can be more or less difficult. But what is achieved in this performance differs essentially from anything that can be done otherwise in a striving action; for here our meaning posits a practical intent.

Now the act of willing also shows a distinctive duality; it is either positive or negative, either a practical affirmation or a practical negation. Certainly, this duality corresponds to the duality of striving and counterstriving, but it is also essentially different from it. It is not a duality of blind reactions but a duality of seeing acts.

So if one compares the act of willing with the strivings, it moves away from them into the sphere of mental (*geistig*) acts. On the other hand, it is different from the purely theoretical acts. For the act of willing itself is not an act of judging that something is or is not the case, that something is or is not valuable, or that something ought or ought not to be. In short, the act of willing is neither a positive nor a negative act of judging about being, value, or oughtness. It may imply such judgments. But none of these acts of judging is itself an act of will. In the acts of judging something is asserted or recognized; in the acts of willing, however, something is willed. Accordingly, the act of willing is also no mere theoretical affirmation or negation. Just as little is a theoretical assent per se an act of willing. In certain circumstances the performance of judgments on being, value, or oughtness is itself a voluntary action, but that does not make these judgments themselves acts of willing. As theoretical propositions (*Sätze*), these judgments are not practical intents (*Vorsätze*).

2. Characteristics of the Act of Willing

ACCORDING TO WHAT WAS SAID ABOVE, the act of willing is that peculiar, purely inner act which precedes the voluntary action and may form the beginning of such an action. It is expressed verbally in sentences of the form "I will" and "I will not." True, one can also interpret these sentences in a different sense, namely, in the sense of predications about the ego and its willing. Then they would be merely special cases of the more general sentences "S will X" and "S will not X," and thus they would be the expression of theoretical judgments, only with a state of affairs of a special kind. But actually those sentences have a different sense: they are the expression of intents (*Vorsätze*) or *voluntaria;* instead of the copula or affirmation of theoretical judgments, here we have the copula of will of practical acts of intent. Whereas the copula of affirmation gives the stamp of positing (*Setzungsgepräge*) to the projected state of affairs, the copula of will imposes the stamp of proposing (*Vorsetzungsgepräge*) on the projected state of affairs.

In performing an act of willing the ego proposes to itself a certain way of behaving of its own, namely, to do something or not to do something. The proposed behavior of the self is to be called the *project*. Thus a first part of the performance of the act of will is the intent of the will (*Willensmeinung*) or the consciousness of the project (*Projektsbewusstsein*) which aims at a certain future behavior of one's own ego. For some reason the proposed personal behavior is then considered valuable; hence, there is a positive valuation of what the voluntary intention is aiming at. At times there is an additional consciousness of oughtness, the opinion or the knowledge that one's own behavior thus conceived ought to be. This oughtness may then be acknowledged, the projected behavior may be approved, and both may occur in acts of acknowledgment and approval, neither of which is an act of the judging intellect. But as long as only the factors thus far mentioned are present, the essential and decisive element, in order to transform the whole situation into a performance of an act of willing, is still missing. For what is still absent is the characteristic practical proposing. This proposing issues from the ego-center, not as an occurrence but as a peculiar doing in which the ego-center centrifugally, from inside itself, performs a mental stroke. This stroke does more than merely approve. By it the meant behavior of the self is proposed but not yet actually executed.

The act of willing refers to one's own ego. If it is not to be one of those pseudo-acts of willing which refer to a severed fantasy ego, if it is to be a genuine act of willing, then one's own ego must not be merely thought about but must itself be immediately grasped and must be made a subject referent [13] of a practical proposing. Thus willing, but not striving, includes the immediate consciousness of self.

13. The terminology of this paragraph uses distinctions which are fully developed in Pfänder's *Logik, Gesammelte Schriften* (Tübingen, 1963), chap II, par. 1, pp. 38 ff. Pfänder distinguishes here between subject-concept (*Subjektsbegriff*) and predicate-concept (*Prädikatsbegriff*), as constituents of the logical proposition (*Urteil*), and subject-referent (*Subjektsgegenstand*) and predicate-referent (*Prädikatsgegenstand*), as constituents of the ontological state of affairs (*Sachverhalt*) projected by the proposition. The copula of the proposition, in addition to its assertive function (*Behauptungsfunktion*), either, in the case of the positive proposition, makes subject-referent and predicate-referent one (*In-eins-setzung*), or, in the case of the negative proposition, sets them apart (*Absetzung*) (chap. VI). This paragraph indicates the kind of science of practical intents or *voluntaria* of which Pfänder speaks in the Appendix.—Trans.

The act of willing is, therefore, a *practical act of proposing filled with a certain intent of the will* which issues from the ego-center and, penetrating to the ego itself, induces in it a certain future behavior. It is an act of self-determination in the sense that the ego is both the subject and the object of the act.

Now the act of willing is either positive or negative, that is, one's own ego as subject referent is either "set-at-one" (*in-eins-gesetzt*) by one's will with an intended future doing of one's own, or "set-apart" by it. In either case, the copula of the will, like the copula of assertion in judgments, has a double function: namely, the function of setting-at-one (or setting-apart), and the function of willing, of which the second is superimposed in a fusion upon the first (*Verschmelzung*).

Now, the practical proposing can be problematic, as in wishing, or hypothetical, as in hypothetical willing. However, in true, genuine willing the proposing is a real and unconditional positing of the will.

If we extract in thought the combined intent of the will and the function of proposing from the performance of the act of willing, we obtain the intent as proposed, or the *voluntarium*. By the performance of a genuine act of willing, the ego is charged with a certain intent. To this extent the act of willing is, therefore, also an act of self-charging (*Selbstladeakt*); the ego charges itself with an intent. The charge thus self-created then either can be brought to release by newly added initiating impulses (*Willensimpulse*), or it can persist *actually* without discharge, or it also may last *virtually* until it either finds its fulfilling discharge at a later time, or evaporates without discharge, or is voluntarily cancelled.

3. The Act of Choosing

THE ACT OF CHOOSING is a special case of the act of willing. It is neither simply a striving nor the "victory" of a striving. Instead of one project it has several mutually exclusive projects before it. After reflection of a longer or shorter duration concerning the objective and subjective possibility, the value, and the oughtness of these different projects, and after a possible weighing of the comparative value and oughtness of the projects, the act of *choice* can then take place. It strikes one of these projects and consists likewise in an act of positive practical proposing, in which the ego proposes to itself the execution of the one project; explicitly or implicitly a variety of negative practical proposings concerning the other projects is simultaneously combined with this act. The difference between a simple act of willing and an act of choosing has nothing at all to do with the number of existing motives. Even a simple act of willing without any choice can have several motives.

Since the act of choosing is also an act of practical proposing, it does not require separate consideration beside the simple act of willing when the nature of the relation of motivation is at stake.

If the act of choosing is really an act of willing, then the mere knowledge or insight that one project is superior in value to other projects, or that it is preferable to the others, may not be called an act of choosing; nor is the mere acknowledgment of the advantages and the approval of the one project in itself an act of choosing.

[III] THE RELATION OF THE ACT OF WILLING TO WHAT "PRECEDES" IT

1. The Relation of the Act of Willing to the Strivings

BEFORE THE ACT OF WILLING is performed and even during its performance there can occur in the same inner life one or several strivings which are directed toward or against the execution of the intended project in question. From the preceding discussions it can be seen that none of these strivings, not even the one which is "victorious" over the opposing strivings, can be identical with the act of willing. The difference of the act of willing from the strivings is also shown in what follows.

A positive act of willing can be directed toward a project against whose execution the ego feels in itself a counterstriving down to the last moment. There are cases in which the ego, with violent counterstriving and in spite of this counterstriving, decides *for* something. In such cases one cannot find any trace of a positive striving which surpasses in strength and conquers the violent counterstriving. In any case the situation is different from the one just mentioned, when the act of willing is carried out in accord with a positive striving which is stronger than a simultaneous counterstriving. In the latter case the total pattern of the striving, in spite of the existing counterstriving, points spontaneously in the direction which the act of willing then also takes.

Secondly, a negative act of willing with regard to a project can be performed, whose execution is a goal of a present positive striving or a positive resultant of strivings. Here, in spite of violent striving toward something, the ego decides against the execution of the project. Even in this case not-willing must not be confused with a counterstriving.

Finally, according to my own experience and that of others, there are acts of willing in whose performance neither strivings toward nor counterstrivings against the projects in question can be discovered. These are especially the cases where, after completely calm and reasonable consideration and insight, one decides for or against something in accordance with this insight. I must consider it a prejudice in favor of a false theory of the will if it is asserted that the strivings which one cannot discover here at all are nevertheless present and that the voluntary decision of the will *consists* in their "victory."

2. The Influence of the Strivings on the Performance of the Act of Willing

THERE IS, HOWEVER, no doubt that the strivings which are present in the ego at a given moment can influence the ego in its performance of acts of willing to a greater or lesser degree and in many cases actually do influence it.

The strivings and counterstrivings which occur are first [merely] incentives (*Anreize*) for the ego, which is capable of willing to perform voluntary actions with respect to these strivings. But beyond this they also incline the ego to decide in favor of the strivings that happen to be present. As to the former case, it is certain that at a given moment the ego would frequently not take voluntary action unless just those specific strivings and counterstrivings occurred in it. Thus I would not propose to buy flowers now unless at this moment the sight of flowers had aroused in me a striving to possess them. The ego which, to be sure, is assumed to be capable of willing is in such cases certainly "induced" to a willing by the existing strivings, and they "determine" the ego not only to a willing in general but to a willing with a specific content. Not only would the ego perhaps not have made a decision at all, but it was even less likely to do so with regard to these projects, unless just these strivings had turned up. If it is true that the ego is to this extent determined by the strivings, that need not "induce" it to a positive or to a negative act of willing. For instance, if a positive striving for something is present, the act of willing which takes place need not by any means be positive in the direction of this striving, that is, it need not by any means be such an act as implies the satisfaction of this striving. As was stressed above, a negative act of willing can be enacted in the presence of a positive striving and in spite of this striving.

In these cases the relation of the strivings to the performance of the act of willing is a phenomenal relation of causation—the ego experiences an urging or pulling coming from the striving, which attacks the ego-center and tries to draw it into the striving. At the same time, and without its doing, a project is visualized, and a readiness to will, as a definite psychological state, is sensibly aroused in it by the striving. In any case, these relations of the strivings to the performance of the act of will are different from those relations which are to be considered in what follows and designated as relations of motivation.

Besides, in immediate experience it is by no means the case that the strivings by themselves simply cause the performance of a certain act of willing. This is excluded by the very essence of the performance of an act of willing. For in experience the ego itself always appears as the agent that performs the act of willing. Never can the performance of an act of willing be a happening which is suffered by the ego; for in that case that which would have taken place would be no longer an act of willing. The peculiar nature of the act of willing is the reason why phenomenally it can be performed only by the ego itself.

Looking back upon previously performed acts of willing, the ego, to be sure, sometimes can establish the fact that at a given time it had permitted itself to be misled or seduced into the performance of those acts of willing by strivings which it just happened to have. ("The flowers were really not that beautiful; I only let myself be seduced into buying them by a violent longing for them.") But even the very expressions "seduce" and "mislead," which in German one usually employs in such cases, point to the fact that here the strivings were not the causes which simply brought about the decision of the will. And the phenomenological consideration of the psychic facts themselves confirms the picture to which these linguistic expressions point. Only one must not be blind to the finer shades of the facts or secretly resist their recognition.

Also, strivings which seduce or mislead us to the performance of certain acts of willing must not be called motives of decisions of the will, if one calls a motive that which stands in a differently constituted relation to the decisions of the will, a relation which will be discussed presently. This stipulation makes it understandable why in men with a sensitive conscience, in all cases in which the decision of their will takes the direction of their present striving, a doubt easily arises as to whether instead of letting themselves be determined by adequate motives they have not let themselves be misled by the existing striving. So too the contrast between the determination of the will by duty and its determination by inclination includes the essential difference between determinations by motives and seduction by strivings.

The act of choosing, as compared with a simple act of willing, does not present anything essentially new with regard to the principle of its relation to the existing strivings. The act of choosing, too, does not always agree with the strongest striving in any given case; in fact no such consonant striving need be present. The act of choosing can also be occasioned (*veranlasst*) or "determined" by existing strivings, but that does not make it simply the effect of the strivings nor motivated by them.

3. The Grounds of the Act of Willing: Motives (*Willensgründe*)

FIRST, LET US CITE a few examples in which something can be a ground of the decision of the will in a special sense, quite different from the cases thus far considered. This relation of the ground to the decision of the will is not put into it by the interpretation of an outside observer but is experienced in the actual facts, hence is present in them phenomenally.

A person enters a room, perceives the chill in it, and decides *on the basis* (*Grund*) *of the perceived chill* to leave the room. A person receives from another a piece of work he had ordered; he recognizes that it has been done with special care, and he decides, *on the basis of the recognized fact* that the other has done the work so carefully, to give him a special reward. A man remembers that when he lived in a certain region he was always very well, and he decides *on the basis of the remembered facts* to revisit that region. A fourth person decides to forego an action on the basis of the thought that another person could feel hurt by this action.

In all these cases acts of willing are performed. In the first case, the perception of the chill prevailing in the room is essential. Attention, apperception, and factual knowledge may be combined with this perception. But this does not exhaust the situation; the mere simultaneity of perception and of the performance of the act of willing does not make the perceived chill a ground of the act of willing.

In the second case, aside from the performance of the act of willing, the perception of the piece of work is essential; so are the cognition of value with regard to the product and the opinion (*Seinsmeinung*) that the other person has created this valuable piece by his special care. But here too the mere simultaneous presence of these facts does not exhaust the situation.

The third and fourth cases are analogous. The performance of the concordant act of willing is matched here by the recollection of certain facts and there by the thought of a future possibility; perhaps cognitions or opinions about value are also present. But in all this the relation of the act of willing to its ground is still missing. This relation, which in all four cases constitutes an essential element of these bodies of fact, must now be determined in its characteristic nature. The analysis of the first example may serve this purpose.

1 / *The Phenomenal Causation of Mental Listening to Demands*

THE PERCEIVED CHILL acts centripetally upon the ego. Aside from the possibility that it may arouse displeasure and counter-striving, which to be sure is by no means necessary in the given case, it causes the ego-center to turn toward it, not only by noticing and apperceiving, but also by listening inwardly or mentally (*geistig*). This mental listening contains a questioning intent (*Zielung*) or attitude (*Haltung*). However, such questioning intents vary greatly according to the content of the questions.[14]

In this connection only that questioning attitude is relevant which is directed toward a reasoned directive for the ego's behavior and which can be formulated in the question, "What shall I do?" To be sure, the attitude of questioning, with its specific content, is not a deliberately articulated posing of the question just formulated; it simply means that the ego lives in this practical questioning attitude. Thus the perceived chill arouses, at first centripetally, the mental listening which turns back to it centrifugally and is filled with a definite practical questioning attitude.

2 / *The Perceiving* (Vernehmen) *of the Demand;
     Its Recognition and Approval*

INTO THIS LISTENING, hence centripetally and, as an answer to the question-behavior going toward it centrifugally,[15] rings out the demand of the chill, which is heard by the ego-center. There is in this perceiving of the demand for a definite behavior a certain acknowledgment of the demand, but at first there is merely a cognitive acknowledgment, namely, the grasp of a mental pointer toward what I am to do. And the perceived chill is first the ground for this realization insofar as this realization is itself supported by what is perceived. This support too is a factor, directed to what has been perceived, in the phenomenal psychic body of fact. To be sure, here the ground is not the ground of a factual knowledge, nor the ground of a knowledge of value, but the ground of a knowledge of oughtness.

But we have not yet made the perceived chill the basis of a decision

14. Cf. Lipps, *op. cit.*, pp. 26, 189.
15. Although the word *"zentripetal"* occurs in the first printing of this text both times, I believe that the second time it should read *zentrifugal.*—Trans.

of the will. For the decision of the will is no mere knowledge of oughtness. Even if the approval of the acknowledged oughtness is added—to be expressed, for example, in the form, "Well, I really ought to do this"—an act of willing has not yet been performed, and the perceived chill has not yet become a ground of willing.

3 / The Performance of the Act of Willing and Its Support on the Ground

AN ENTIRELY DIFFERENT, a genuinely practical acknowledgment has to be added to the knowing and approving acknowledgment of the demand in its specific content if the perceived chill is really to become a ground of willing. This practical acknowledgment consists first in the performance of the act of willing by which the ego resolves upon what is demanded. But this resolving could happen without having the perceived chill supply the ground for it. Even if a demand is recognized and approved, and even if the resolving takes place and can actually count as a certain fulfillment of the demand, the ego's resolving need not happen *on the ground* of the demand. This is true universally: possible grounds for a certain willing, even if the ego is actually conscious of them and their demand, need not be grounds out of which the ego performs this definite willing; they may even be expressly eliminated as grounds in the performing of the act of willing.

Only then does the perceived chill really become the ground for the act of willing, when the ego, in performing the act of willing, uses the demanding chill as its support, when it grounds the act of willing on the demand and "educes" (*eduziert*) it from the demand. Not until then is the relation of grounding (*Begründungsbeziehung*) complete. At that stage the ego has no longer left the demand standing outside and has no longer merely acknowledged and approved of it, but has taken it in, has incorporated it, and has then, in falling back upon it, carried out the act of willing in accordance with the demand and thus fulfilled it ideally for the time being. This using something as support in the performance of an act of willing is a peculiar mental doing. Only by this mental support is the connection between ground and act of willing established, and only thus does the possible ground become a real ground of willing.

Quite similar to the first example considered is the situation in the three other examples. The known fact that the other has done his job so carefully demands of the ego which is ready to listen a special rewarding of the other. The ego receives this demand and approves of it; it performs the act of willing to give a special reward to the other by using the demanding fact as support and by this supporting act of the will takes the first step toward the practical acknowledgment of the demand by action. In the third example, the remembered facts are posited as the ground, and in the fourth example, the thought of the possibility that another person could feel hurt by a certain deed functions as ground for the negative act of willing to forego the action in question.

In all these cases one uses the word "motive" in order to say that something was the ground of a decision of will. One calls the perceived chill the motive for the resolve to leave the room; the known fact that the other has done the job so carefully is called the motive for the decision to give him a special reward; the remembered fact that I always felt very well while staying in a certain region is called the motive for the decision to revisit this region; and the thought that another person could feel hurt by my conduct is the motive for the decision to forego this conduct. And indeed, it might be expedient to use the word "motive" only in this sense of the demanding ground of willing and accordingly to understand by motivation only that peculiar relation which exists between a demanding ground of willing and the act of willing supported by it.

[IV] THE DISTINCTION OF MOTIVATION FROM OTHER RELATIONS

1. The Making of Practical Demands and the Arousal of Strivings

ONE MIGHT THINK that when it is said of the perceived chill that it makes the practical demand to leave the room, this does not mean anything but the arousal of positive striving to leave the room. One could support this idea by pointing out that in both cases a stimulus moves centripetally from the confronting chill toward the ego. But although this pointer is correct, the posing of practical demands is essentially different from the stimulation of strivings. This difference is seen in the following ways:

(1) The perceived chill can arouse a counterstriving in the ego without the simultaneous development of a practical demand upon the ego. This is the case, for instance, when an individual is involved in concentrated mental work and incidentally perceives the chill prevailing in the room. Then a constant counterstriving against the chill can be aroused, and this counterstriving can remain in a remote corner of

the ego, as it were, without the ego's hearing a practical demand issuing from the chill. Perhaps the chill even arouses that questioning listening previously mentioned; but then this listening bypasses the chill in the wrong direction, as it were, and receives no kind of demanding answer. But if in this case strivings can be aroused without simultaneous demands being made, then strivings and demands are necessarily different things.

(2) Carrying further the example just given: it can happen that suddenly the perceived chill enters the direction of the questioning listening and now in answering makes its practical demand. Here the previously existing arousal of the counterstriving clearly departs from the new additional making of a practical demand.

(3) The same difference emerges from the fact that the perceived chill can make the practical demand to leave the room without arousing any negative or positive striving. If the chill is not very intense and is perceived at once on entering the room, a consciousness completely free from striving can arise in the face of the chill: "I really ought to leave this room" (the chill makes the demand to leave the room, and the ego perceives this demand without feeling any kind of striving for or against). This is a case of "purely rational insight," which takes place without striving.

(4) The perceived chill can always make the same practical demand while simultaneously the aroused counterstriving increases or diminishes in its intensity. And it makes a positive demand while it arouses a negative striving. In other cases something makes a negative demand while it arouses simultaneously a positive striving.

All this points to the difference which exists between the making of practical demands and the arousal of strivings. The difference itself can be characterized in the following manner:

(5) The arousal of strivings is a phenomenal causal action going on in a centripetal direction. The making of a practical demand, however, penetrates into a perceiving attitude that comes to meet it from the ego and is a non-real (*ideell*) pointing. The strivings are real facts; the demands are non-real pointers.

(6) The arousal befalls the ego; it touches or seizes the ego. And the ego suffers the aroused strivings like a compulsion of nature. By contrast the ego perceives the demands made upon it. It is not conquered by them but confronts them in complete freedom.

(7) The regions of the soul which are engaged in the two cases, the arousal of strivings and the making of demands, are different. The arousal affects the "body of the soul" (*Seelenleib*), as it were, whereas the making of the demand addresses the "spirit of the soul" (*Seelengeist*) and specifically that part of the "spirit" of the soul which

is able to hear the practical demands made by this "spirit." In certain cases this inner hearing [16] (*geistiges Gehör*) for practical demands can be deaf or merely benumbed, it can be exhausted or fatigued, or finally, involuntarily or voluntarily, it can be merely turned off. Then the ego does not perceive any practical demands, or it merely hears them indistinctly and weakly, while at the same time it may be seized by violent and distinctly felt strivings and counterstrivings.

It follows even from the difference between the arousal of strivings and the making of demands as here demonstrated that nothing can be a motive in any way as long as it arouses merely strivings. But even when something makes a practical demand perceived by the ego, it is not yet a real motive but only a possible one.

2. Motivation and Phenomenal Stimulation. Motives and Stimuli

AS WAS SAID EARLIER, phenomenally the arousal of strivings can have a character very different [from motivation], namely, that of an attracting or repelling stimulation or that of a release of drives in the ego aiming toward or away [from a thing]. In the former case the object which arouses the striving appears as the starting point of a pulling or repelling which attacks the ego. This phenomenal pulling and repelling differs too from the making of practical demands. It is not a motivating, even if it has the result that the strivings are satisfied. Motives must therefore be carefully distinguished from stimuli or incentives in this phenomenal sense. To be determined by motives is something entirely different from being attracted or repelled by incentives.

3. Motives and Drives

IN THE LATTER CASE, where the aroused strivings have the character of drives within the ego, the starting point of the striving or counterstriving appears to be an eccentric spot in the ego. These strivings with the character of drives can take effect involuntarily until fulfillment. For instance, while a person engaged in a fascinating

16. I have rendered *geistiges Hinhören* by "inner listening" instead of the more literal "spiritual listening," because in English "spirit," and even more, "spiritual," have too many connotations, not only Hegelian but purely religious, which are absent from ordinary German and also from Pfänder's way of thinking. In fact, Pfänder, who in his earlier writings often described the psyche as a living being with a body, a "soul," and a "spirit," abandoned in his last work on *Man's Psyche* (*Die Seele des Menschen*) (Halle, 1933) the term *Geist* completely, since the word still has "a very indefinite meaning" (p. 4).—Trans.

conversation is answering his partner, the sight of a little piece of candy on his plate arouses in him the drive to eat it; he seizes the morsel and consumes it. Here the drive is the phenomenal cause of the action, but the action is no action of the will, and the drive cannot be called the motive of the action. Drives as such, insofar as they do not make practical demands and are not made conscious supports for an act of willing, may have all sorts of effects phenomenally and perhaps even really, but then they do not motivate and therefore are to be distinguished strictly from motives. To be determined by motives is not the same thing as to be driven by drives. The two things belong in completely different spheres.

4. Motives and Sources of Striving

THERE IS AN EXPERIENCED ISSUANCE of striving from another psychic experience, for instance, from pleasure or displeasure or from another striving. Thus it can be experienced that the striving to drink water is the origin of the striving to seize the glass in which the water is contained. As has already been done, one can call that from which striving issues in our experience the phenomenal source of striving. Then this issuance of a striving from its phenomenal source is obviously different from the previously characterized motivation of an act of willing by certain motives. And the motives are not to be confused with mere sources of a striving or counterstriving.

5. Motives and Sources of Willing

THE SOURCE from which the performance of the act of will issues phenomenally is always the ego-center itself. This is based upon the essential nature of willing. When this issuance from the ego-center is missing, no act of willing can be performed at all. Hence, motives cannot be the phenomenal sources of willing. At most one could call the motives the non-real (*ideell*) sources of the volitional intent (*Vorsatz*). But the intent receives the stamp of the will not from the motive but exclusively from the ego-center.

6. Motives and Causes of Willing

IT IS PROBABLE that motives have been most frequently confused with the *causes* of willing. The question as to the causes of willing may be understood first phenomenologically, that is, we may ask the question as to what is experienced, in performing an act of will, as the cause of this performance. From this question in the particular case we can obtain with self-evidence the general answer that the phenomenal cause of the performance of an act of the will is never anything outside the ego-center but is always the ego-center itself. The entire essential nature of this willing would be immediately destroyed if any kind of a phenomenal cause outside the ego-center caused the supposed willing. In particular, the consideration of the phenomenal position taken by the motive with regard to the performance of the act of willing which uses it as support yields the evident knowledge that in no case does the motive *cause* this performance. Without this support of the act of willing by the motive, one which issues from the ego-center itself, the possible motive in a given case is not the real motive for this act of willing. With this support, to be sure, the motive does become "determining" for the willing. However, the determination by motives is after all no phenomenal causation by motives at all, the grounding of the will (*Willensbegründung*) is no causation of willing, and motives are no phenomenal causes of willing. It is a contradiction of the facts, therefore, when Schopenhauer affirms that motivation is causality seen from within.[17] For what is seen "from within" in the case of the determination of the will by motives is completely different from causation. There is no such thing as a phenomenal causation of willing in this sense. According to its essential nature, willing is always free phenomenally; it is not caused by something different from the ego-center.

However, the question as to the causes of willing can have a different sense, for it can ask for the real causes of willing. It then refers to the performance of the act of willing as a real event in time and wants to know the real factors by whose occurrence just at this particular point in time this real event has been brought about. But a phenomenological investigation cannot supply an answer to this question. Instead, on the basis of other kinds of experiences and of inductive methods one has to look for the necessary and sufficient real conditions for the occurrence of willing in the concrete case. The relation of real cause and effect here is not a directly experienced relation. That which is a part of the cause of willing need not have been known to the willing subject, nor does this cause have to make a practical demand perceived by the ego: the cause only must have been really existent at the specific moment. Ultimately it is not a necessary part of the reality of a causal relation that there is a conscious support of the will by what is part of the cause.

All these things, however, which are not necessarily part of a

17. "Über die vierfache Wurzel des Satzes vom zureichenden Grunde." (*Sämtliche Werke* [Wiesbaden, 1948]), I, 144 f.

causal relation, form the necessary and essential conditions for a relation of motivation. So it is certain that the motivational relation differs from the causal relation. But it might still be the case that the motivational relation is a special instance of the causal relation. In fact, the assumption that this is so is frequently made. Wherever one looks for the real cause of an act of will one usually lists unhesitatingly among other contributing causes (*Teilursachen*) the motives as partial causes of willing. At times one actually defines motives as the conscious partial causes of willing. So it is said that motives combined with character are the real causes of willing.

The fact that there is a fundamental error in these assumptions, that the motivational relation is not a causal relation and that therefore motives as motives must never be mingled with causes of willing, follows from the following considerations:

Whatever is to be a part of the real cause of willing must necessarily be something real. By contrast, a motive need not be anything real; rather, something that is merely thought or is merely ideal (*Ideelles*) can be a motive of a willing. For instance, the truth of an assertion can be the motive for my resolving to enunciate this assertion on a given occasion.

Besides, not only must a partial cause be something real in general, but it must also be real at the time when the effect takes place. If, for instance, the fact that someone has carried out a job with particular care or the fact that previously I was always particularly well in a certain region is a motive for my willing, these motives as past facts cannot be partial causes of my willing now. Likewise, future facts can be real motives in anticipation, but as long as they still are in the future they cannot possibly be partial causes. True, one can claim that the thinking of the past or future facts, which is real now, is a partial cause; but it is precisely this real "thinking" which is *not* the motive of my willing.

Finally, it can be recognized by immediate observation that the relation of motive to the act of willing by which that motive is really a motive differs totally from the relation of a partial cause to its proper effect. The motive has no contributing effect at all on the performance of an act of willing but only offers the non-real (*ideell*) support to the ego-center, which alone performs the act of willing.

Thus on principle the *causes* of willing may not be put on the same level with the *motives* of willing, if one wants to avoid the utter confusion which must arise by not paying attention to this essential difference and which actually prevails, for instance, in the studies of the freedom of the will.

7. Motives and Guiding Principles, Rules, Models, Prescriptions, Laws, Commands

LET IT SIMPLY BE POINTED OUT here that besides the motivational relation there are still other characteristic relations between the performance of acts of will and those factors by which the ego-center lets itself be determined. Thus, in forming intents before giving them the stamp of will, the ego can let itself be guided by general principles or rules. In other cases, in executing the act of willing, it performs an *assimilation* to certain models. In its willing, the ego follows intentionally certain prescriptions; it obeys or subjects itself to certain laws or commands. This letting itself be guided, adapting itself, following, obeying, subjecting itself in willing is each time something special and something which really takes place in mental life. To be sure, one has often used these words in psychology, without being consciously aware that they are no mere empty phrases but really mean something. What is meant by these words must be drawn explicitly into the ken of psychology and not only be always carried along tacitly and [left] in the dark. Here an abundance of tasks opens up before phenomenological psychology. To be sure, the idea of the human mind which primitive peoples have (suitable for children's primers) must be left far behind to enable one even to see these tasks.

Those previously mentioned relations, differing from the motivational relation, are also different from one another. This does not exclude the possibility that exactly the same behavior which stands in one relation to willing, say the relation of obedience, can also stand in another relation to it, say the motivational relation.

[V] THE POSSIBILITY AND THE NECESSITY OF MOTIVATION

1. The Possibility of Motivation

SINCE THE MOTIVATIONAL RELATION previously characterized includes the idea that a decision of will is performed and is also supported consciously by a mentally heard demand, the possibility of a motivation is excluded in all those cases in which even one of these factors is missing. If what we have called the performance of an act of willing really does not occur, as for instance in animals, then in animal psychology one must never talk of any animal as having done something from *motives.* Perhaps one must not do this for the mere reason that possibly animals lack that sense of "inner hearing" for demands. However, even in the case of man there can be no motivation when he does not make a decision of willing; or when this decision is not actually supported by what might become a motive and which has made its demand that has been heard internally; or, finally, when the practical demand of the potential motive has not been heard internally at all.

It seems to contradict these conclusions that in several cases the willing individual does not know how to tell the motives by which he has let himself be determined in his willing and that one talks of "unconscious" motives of willing. But one can really do many a thing without being able to tell afterwards what one has done and how one has done it—indeed, without knowing afterwards *that* one has done it. Knowledge and noticing of what one does need not accompany the doing itself. Besides, there is an involuntary repression (*Verdrängen*) from oneself or a concealing from oneself (*Verborgenhalten*) of the real motives and an involuntary pretending or substitution of sham motives by which one supports to oneself the act of willing. One calls not only the forgotten and unnoticed motives but also those inwardly concealed one's "unconscious motives," although of course they are not "unconscious" in every sense of the word. What is unconscious in the genuine sense of the word can never be a motive at all.

2. The Necessity of Motivation

THE CONFUSION OF MOTIVES and causes of willing has led to the assertion that every willing has necessarily a motive from which it proceeds with necessity. As to the first part of this contention, namely, that willing has necessarily a ground of willing, I am not yet able to reach a definite insight. In any case the contention must not mean that each willing has necessarily a ground of willing which lies outside the proposed state of affairs. For frequently a motive can be found, if at all, only within the very project before our eyes. One can want something for its own sake without being determined by any motives lying outside it.

The second part of the contention, namely, that the motives necessarily bring about the willing, must be disputed as invalid in every regard if one really means motives and not causes of willing. To begin with, as was pointed out above, there are cases in which possible motives are conscious; in which their practical demands also are heard inwardly, but in which either no decision of will takes place at all or the decision of will occurs in conflict with the possible motive; or, finally, in which the decision of will is carried out, to be sure, in accord with the practical demand of that motive, but is supported not by it but by entirely other motives. Now if, finally, the act of willing as performed is really supported by the motive in question, two other different cases are possible. The motive can be either completely sufficient or more or less insufficient. The mere existence of insufficiently motivated decisions of the will shows that motives are not the causes of willing. For if the motivation were a causation, insufficiently motivated acts of willing could not really be performed at all.

If, therefore, there has been only an insufficient motive for a performed act of willing, it is immediately certain that this motive did not bring about the willing causally. Even if there was a sufficient motive for the willing and even if the willing actually took place, this motive did not necessarily bring about the willing, because motives do not cause anything; they *supply grounds*. True, the grounding by a sufficient motive has a different character from the one by an insufficient motive. The demand which resounds into the "inner" listening from the sufficient motive and is perceived by the central ego-center is unambiguous and definite, and it is able to uphold the appropriate act of will supported by it entirely by itself, i.e., to give a sufficient ground for it. By contrast, the insufficient motive does not make an unambiguous or definite demand and is by itself not sufficiently able to keep up the appropriate act of willing, if it is supported by this motive. Besides, the ego-center experiences that definite and unambiguous demand perceived as an obligating "spiritual" bond. But this spiritual bond is not causal compulsion. If the ego submits to the "spiritual" bond by performing the required act of willing on the ground of the demand, this process has phenomenally a very different appearance from the one in which the ego succumbs to a causal compulsion. The necessity which is based upon a demand is something different from the necessity which is based on causal action. In the case of the sufficient motive the required act of willing is necessary in the sense of an ought-to-be but not necessary in the sense that its performance was caused by the motive.

Hence, it is true that the sufficient motive makes a certain act of willing a "necessary" one, but it does not make the performance of the act of willing one which necessarily takes place. The sufficient motive too motivates the performance of the act of willing only when the ego-center makes it the support of its willing. Only those possible motives are real motives by which the central ego lets itself be determined. In this sense the ego confronts, freely willing, even completely sufficient motives. Indeed, it can eliminate from motivation even sufficient motives whose demands it perceives and can base the acts of

willing demanded by them on completely different motives and perform them. However, if the ego lets itself be induced by the sufficient
motive to the performance of the demanded act of willing, this letting
itself be determined is something entirely special and essentially different from all causal and necessary action.

3. Willing Follows Necessarily from the Actual Motives and from Character

THE PROPOSITION that not the motives alone, but the
motives jointly with the character of the willing person necessarily
entail willing enjoys widespread recognition, but at the same time also
suffers from an equally widespread misinterpretation. Since motives
as motives do not cause, this proposition must not be understood
causally at all. Indeed, it does not owe its persuasiveness to an empirical causal induction but is fundamentally an analytic proposition, and
the necessity of which it speaks is the analytic necessity according to
which a metal of a certain melting point actually melts at that point.
For the character which is mentioned in that proposition is not by any
means a mere quality with which the willing ego is simply equipped,
but it is, or at least it contains as an essential element, the way in
which the ego makes its volitional decisions when certain motives are
present. Only beings capable of will can have character in this sense.
It is of course an obvious truth that from this character, that is, from
the definite way in which the ego decides voluntarily in the case of
certain motives, the definite willing follows when these definite motives
are actually present in him, a matter which, however, does not settle
the least thing about the real causation of the decision of the will.
Rather, it is presupposed in the concept of character that the freely
willing ego-center is the ultimate cause of the concrete decisions
of the will. For the character is not a thing of a certain quality in
which, on the basis of its quality, in the case of certain influences,
certain effects would take place; it is rather that in the middle of the
character stands the ego-center which wills spontaneously in a certain
manner and is the free doer and not the sufferer of willing.

[VI] APPENDIX

SINCE THERE ARE MOTIVES and motivation in the sense
designated above and since giving grounds for practical intents is
something different from giving grounds for judgments, the vista
opens up of a science of the practical intents or *voluntaria* analogous

to logic. It would have to determine the essence and the structure of the *voluntaria* in general, then the possible kinds of *voluntaria*, moreover, the kinds of motivation for *voluntaria* and the logical connections between different *voluntaria*.

Imperatives form a special kind of *voluntaria*. A theory of imperatives, of which I have drafted a still unpublished sketch, could in my opinion offer a final scientific foundation for ethics, the philosophy of law, and pedagogics. However, right now I cannot elucidate this idea further, but must be content with this mere hint at it.[18]

18. Pfänder never published this draft, and no manuscript among his papers now deposited in the Bayerische Staatsbibliothek in Munich (Pfänderiana), seems to meet this specification. However, the second part of Pfänder's still unpublished ethics (*Kurze Darstellung*) in its treatments of demands (*Forderungen*) contains pertinent discussions.—Trans.

3 / Introduction to *Logic*

THUS FAR PFÄNDER's *Logik*, like most German works on logic since the days of Christoph Sigwart, has attracted little, if any, attention among Anglo-American logicians, although it did among the Spanish-American ones. In part this may be due to the new trend toward symbolic logic, for which only such mathematicians as Eduard Schröder and Gottlob Frege have seemed relevant. Indeed, Pfänder's *Logik* does not go beyond the minimum symbols found in Aristotelian logic, with the addition of some new symbols which he introduced for certain functions of logical thought that had not been described in this manner before.

However, at this time there would be little point in recommending Pfänder's *Logik* as especially pertinent to the concerns of symbolic logicians. In logic, Pfänder's chance may come if and when there should be increased interest in the ontological, if not the metaphysical, meaning of logical symbolism. Then one would discover the similarities between Bertrand Russell's and Wittgenstein's early views about the relation between logic and reality and about propositions and states of affairs, on the one hand, and Pfänder's scheme on the other. But in the present context my main purpose is to introduce Pfänder's conception of logic in relation to his views on phenomenology. For his *Logik* was in a sense the major achievement of phenomenology in the field of systematic logic. Logic as such had, of course, been a special concern of the Phenomenological Movement, beginning with Husserl's laying of the ground by his criticism of psychologism in the interest of pure logic. However, the second volume of his *Logical Investigations* contained only disconnected preparations for such an enterprise, pioneering though these studies were. Even when Husserl returned to the field in his *Formal and Transcendental Logic* of 1929, this was not a system of either of these two types of logic but was mostly a program for the development of these two complementary enterprises. Pfänder's *Logik* is, therefore, the first and only systematic treatise on formal logic as it was conceived by Husserl in his early period. This claim can be supported by the historical fact that in 1909, on the occasion of a visit to Munich, Husserl asked Pfänder to write a textbook on logic, presumably in accord with Husserl's conceptions at this time. It took Pfänder until 1921 before this text was completed. He then dedicated it to Husserl on the occasion of his sixtieth birthday. It also contains a special reference to Husserl as the classic critic of psychologism (refuted even more succinctly by Pfänder), the only explicit tribute in this work. But implicitly Pfänder refers repeatedly to Husserl's account of thought and its "intentional" structure. There is, however, no evidence that Husserl was particularly impressed by Pfänder's work. In fact, in a card which I received from Husserl in June, 1936, he stated that to him "Pfänder's psychology and even his logic, though they were serious pieces of work, constituted as little philosophy as any work in the sciences."

Regardless of the merits of Pfänder's *Logik* in Husserl's later perspective, its "scientific" claim can be defended on its own rights. But this is not the task of these introductory remarks. They are merely intended to prepare the ground for a proper understanding of the following selection. And since this selection is Pfänder's own Introduction, it should be able to speak for itself. What does make sense is to convey a first idea of some of the features (and particularly the original features) of the main body of the book. The last section of Pfänder's Introduction outlines the sequence of the topics taken up in the subsequent text, yet without advertising its original contributions. In the present context, however, it is well to point out some of the major concepts in Pfänder's discussion in view of their potential relevance for present-day logic.

The first section dealing with the doctrine of judgment begins with a preparatory sub-section in which the threefold stratification of logic is outlined, consisting of (1) the linguistic sentence, differing from language to language; (2) the proposition, which is the same for all of them; and (3) the state of affairs, expressible through different propositions. The elements of the proposition are distinguished, and the two different functions of the copula (connection of subject and predicate, and assertion) are pointed out. In the further study and classification of judgments, their relations to different types of states of affairs are explored.

The section dealing with concepts characterizes these in their intermediate position between words and objects meant. Various new ways of classifying concepts are developed. Perhaps the most original section examines and groups the "purely functioning" (*rein funktionierend*) concepts in contrast to those which are "object-referring" (*gegenstandsbezogen*). I am not familiar with any other attempt to describe and group the so-called "syncategorematics" as thoroughly and illuminatingly as do these sections of Pfänder's text.

Pfänder's undertaking, in the third section, to save the fundamental logical laws from triviality and to justify them in this clarified sense is remarkable chiefly for its attempt to reinterpret them as laws about the truth and falsehood of propositions and to find their foundation in the ontic "behavior of things" (*Verhalten der Dinge*).

Pfänder's study of the doctrine of inferences starts from the traditional Aristotelian theory of direct and indirect inferences but criticizes it sharply. It also tries to derive their valid forms from the essential nature of the ontic states of affairs. The last sections contain some original suggestions about inductive inferences, inference by analogy, and inferences based on material relations, all trying to find their foundations in the ontic sphere.

Thus one of the major results of Pfänder's study of formal logic is its dependence on formal ontology, about which the book contains some very important insights. While I submit that a good many of these motifs were not only original at the time but may still be of value in the present and future condition of logic, the major question in the present context is their relationship to Pfänder's conception of phenomenology.

Here a first look, especially at Pfänder's explicit discussion of phenomenology in the fifth section of the translated Introduction, may give the impression that the fields of logic and phenomenology differ, phenomenology stressing the subjective aspects of experience and studying thoughts only as the intentional referents of the subject's thinking, logic concentrating on the thoughts for their own sake and by themselves. Thus Pfänder seems to see in phenomenology merely a complement to logic, at least if logic should also include the study of the relation of thought to the acts of thinking in their phenomenological structure. One can well imagine that this role of phenomenology did not satisfy Husserl, who was already in search of a transcendental foundation for logic in phenomenology.

What must not be overlooked, however, is that the conception of phenomenology toward which Pfänder was cautiously moving was by no means the one which was shared by all the members of the older Phenomenological Movement when Pfänder was working on this book. At that time, the time of the phenomenological "platform" which headed the first volume of the yearbook, phenomenology stood primarily for the principles of intuitive verification (*Anschauung*) and essential insights (*Wesenseinsicht*). Seen in this light practically all of Pfänder's *Logik* is phenomenological. This is particularly true of the early parts of the Introduction with their stress on the variety of phenomena in the field of thinking with its intentional referents and the manyfold thoughts, in addition to those studied by traditional logic, on which Pfänder was to concentrate in the main body of the text. All through the book, Pfänder's patient attempt to show concretely the referents of all thoughts by way of objects, real or non-real (*ideell*), and functions and to give insight into all the propositions and laws of logic certainly fulfills the demands of intuitive verification. Besides, he constantly tries to find not only contingent but essentially necessary connections among the thoughts and their foundations in ontic facts and between logical thoughts among themselves. Thus, if phenomenology is the science of essences, it is more than justified that Pfänder's *Logik* passed and still passes among many as *the* logic text of phenomenology.

Finally, a connection could easily be established between Pfänder's method in the *Logik* and recent "linguistic phenomenology." Throughout the main text of the *Logik*, Pfänder stresses over and over again the need to first clarify the ordinary meaning of a term or sentence before checking on its truth (cf. pp. 50, 69 f.). In fact, all through the book Pfänder begins his discussion with the elimination of misinterpretations of the ordinary meanings of terms and sentences prior to the examination of their right or justification. It may go too far to speak here of linguistic analysis. But Pfänder's approach to logic fits in particularly well with this more recent philosophy; in fact, it goes far beyond it in its subsequent analysis of the phenomena.—H. S.

[I] Subject Matter and Task of Logic

According to an old and still widespread definition, logic is the study of thinking. This definition is not completely wrong; for indeed the subject matter of logic lies in thinking. But all the same, the definition is not accurate and is at least lopsided. For it is not thinking itself, this psychic process or this mental (*geistig*) activity, but rather something which lies within thinking which is the proper subject matter of logic. The inadequacy of that old definition became manifest in the nineteenth century, when it was taken literally and people really wanted to convert logic into a study of thinking. For in this way they got involved in the domain of psychology, which naturally has to investigate thinking along with other psychic processes too. Logic was in danger of being swallowed up by psychology and being demoted into one of its chapters. To be sure, it was sensed that logic was and is not simply a psychology of thinking; yet, in clinging to that old definition and continuing to hold up to it thinking as its subject matter, people now struggled frantically to free logic from the entanglement with psychology. Two different approaches were taken in order to do justice to the peculiar nature of logic.

The first approach starts from the distinction between theoretical and practical sciences and implies that logic as the practical science of thinking can be properly and correctly separated from psychology as the theoretical science of thinking. However, it soon turned out that while in this way one defect of the definition could be remedied and that the science so defined was secured against absorption by psychology, this led to a new predicament. For logic never really had been a practical science. Hence, as soon as it made this new claim, it had to face the charge of total uselessness.

The second approach likewise sticks to the thesis that logic has thinking as its subject matter and seeks to dislodge it from psychology by assigning to it the task of a normative science of thinking, while it assigns to psychology the task of a factual science of thinking. Whereas psychology is to find out how human thinking *actually* proceeds, logic is to determine how this thinking *ought* to proceed. However, even this characterization conflicted with the essential nature of logic as it actually existed and did not result in a neat separation from psychology.

Both attempts suffered from the fundamental defect which stemmed from that old definition, inasmuch as it continued to determine thinking as the subject matter of logic. Actually, the texts in logic, except in their introductions, did not talk about thinking at all, neither as it actually is nor as it ought to be. Thus the impression remained that so far logic had not yet succeeded in defining clearly and adequately its subject matter and its task.

Now in order to isolate the proper subject matter of logic we shall follow, on the one hand, the directive of this definition by turning toward thinking, analyzing it briefly into its distinguishable factors and looking in it for what has not yet been examined by any other science. Then we shall pay attention, on the other hand, to what kind of objects, in the last analysis, have always been the targets of logic as it actually exists. It then will turn out that that directive and this attempt converge on a distinctive area of objects, which is precisely the one to which logic as a theoretical science must turn.

Thinking is a real psychic occurrence which certainly is found in all wakeful adult human individuals. In every single case that we might investigate a series of five factors can be distinguished in thinking. First, it contains a thinking subject from which thinking starts or by which it is performed. Secondly, thinking itself as a real psychic occurrence which begins at a certain moment in time lasts for a period and then ceases again. Thirdly, in every such thinking a certain idea (*Gedanke*) is thought which forms the thought content (*Gedankengehalt*). Fourthly, in people who have command of a language, this thought content is always expressed or clothed more or less completely and accurately in certain linguistic forms. Fifthly, the thinking subject, thinking, and the thought content dressed in language always refer to some object (*Gegenstand*) in the most general sense of the word. Now these factors are interwoven by a tissue of peculiar relations into a whole whose structure we shall explore a little further.

Let us first consider the relation in which the thinking subject and thinking stand to each other. The thinking subject can exist by itself, even when it happens not to be thinking. It does not necessarily have to think in order to exist. Mostly, to be sure, it does think even when other psychic occurrences such as loving or hating, desiring or willing happen to occupy it. Even if the subject cannot exist without psychic life, it does not necessarily have to think and has, therefore, to this extent a certain freedom in relation to thinking.

However, thinking cannot exist at all without being the thinking of a certain psychic subject. It cannot be separated from the thinking subject whose thinking it is without itself dissolving. The thinking of one subject cannot be separated from it and cannot be transferred to another subject. Every single thinking in order to be real must necessarily belong to one and only one subject. The subject is the only source and the necessary starting point of thinking.

In the other direction, thinking necessarily has content. A thinking which would have no thought content at all, an "empty" thinking in this sense, is impossible. Thinking produces the thought content; it spins it out, builds it up, or copies it. The thought products (*Gedankengebilde*) formed by thinking are "preserved" in thinking; they have real existence only in and with thinking itself. But, on the other hand, they can be separated, in a certain sense, from the thinking which has produced them and transmitted to another thinking. Precisely the same thought which the one thinking subject has thought can be handed down by communication to a second and a third thinking subject and be thought by them too. Besides, thoughts can be put down in writing by the subject who thinks them and thus seemingly can acquire a being outside any thinking subject. However, even the thoughts thus transmitted and put down in writing are really in existence only when they are thought by a thinking subject. Despite this intimate union which thoughts maintain with thinking, they differ from thinking. For whereas thinking is a real psychic occurrence, thoughts are not real psychic occurrences but are idea-like (*ideelle*) timeless products (*Gebilde*). They are spiritual (*geistige*) products of life, which are part of a purely idea-like sphere.

Now thinking can produce thoughts without their being at the same time expressed, put down, proclaimed, or formulated in any linguistic form. Thoughts are by no means necessarily dependent for their being upon linguistic expressions. Actually in every man's thinking there is a mute or quiet thinking which does not find expression in either outward or inward speaking. In many cases the linguistic formulation of a thought takes place only when the thought to be formulated has already been thought in a peculiarly global manner and is at the same time further held fast while the linguistic formulation is carried out successively in time. Even in those cases in which thinking is accompanied from the start by an inner speaking, the thoughts that are thought are rarely clothed fully and completely in words but remain largely unexpressed. The thread of thought spun out in solitary thinking, therefore, usually is covered by linguistic material not along its entire length but only here and there, intermittently, as if by a broken crust. Finally, even where in communicative thinking complete linguistic sentences are formed orally or in writing, the thought content is not expressed exhaustively in these sentences; hence, the listener or reader must figure out by lucky guess its unexpressed content, if he is to absorb it completely. Just as little as thoughts in general are necessarily tied to a linguistic expression, just as little is any definite thought chained to a definite linguistic expression. Rather, one and the same thought can be expressed in different linguistic forms not only in the same language but also more or less accurately in quite different languages. Thus thoughts, in their relation to the linguistic forms, have a certain degree of leeway.

On the other hand, the spoken patterns too need not necessarily have the same thought content. Speech sounds can be produced or picked up purely by themselves without being connected with thoughts. Likewise, one can produce or pick up in reading written symbols quite thoughtlessly. Here the written symbols may have a sense of their own or be completely empty of meaning.

It is clearly evident from these situations that thoughts are different from spoken expressions and must be distinguished from them even when the thoughts appear in a linguistic garb which covers them completely.

The expressive relation which can exist between thoughts and certain linguistic expressions is not a mere simultaneous presence of thoughts and linguistic forms in one and the same consciousness but a relation of a very special kind. In a given case certain speech sounds can be present in a consciousness, while at the same time definite thoughts are thought, and yet those sounds are not the expression of those thoughts. This is the case, for example, when one hears the speech sounds of an unfamiliar language and at the same time, with the aid of one's own mother tongue, thinks such thoughts as are in no way expressed by sounds of the foreign language. In that case speech sounds filled with thoughts coexist with those without them, and the difference of the expressive relation from the mere simultaneity of coexistence becomes clearly visible. This relation is not a reversible one; although the thoughts are expressed in the speech forms, the converse is not the case, i.e., that the speech forms are expressed in thoughts. The thoughts are imbedded in the speech forms as their meaning. They can be grasped in the speech forms only by those persons who have learned the language in question and in the given case turn to the speech sounds with a thought sphere so opened up that the thoughts corresponding to the speech sounds can develop.

Necessarily, thinking and thoughts always are related to objects. Thinking without objects and, likewise, thoughts which have no relation at all to objects are not only actually non-existent, but they are completely impossible, because it is part of their innermost essential nature to have such relations. But thinking and thoughts are by no means confined to definite kinds of objects. Rather is their possible range of objects in principle completely unlimited. They can refer to any category of objects. Not only any kind of thing but also any kinds of states or properties of things, any kinds of processes, activities, effects, relations, and situations can be the objects of thinking and thoughts.

The objects of thinking and thoughts can belong to any area of objects. All areas of reality are in principle open to thinking. The material world of lifeless objects, the world of embodied living beings, the psychic world, the social world, the cultural world, and the world of religious objects—they all present themselves to thinking as its possible objects. All *non-real* (*irreale*) objects, the timeless as well as the fictitious, are accessible to reference in the thinking performance of thoughts. So there is in principle nothing at all that could not become somehow an object of a thinking or a thought.

Now whereas thinking and thoughts never can be without an object to which they refer, the objects by themselves are by no means necessarily dependent on any thinking or any thoughts. They are not at all affected or influenced in their being by the thinking which points to them. Nor does an object of any kind admit only this or that thought referring to it; it can be the object of an unlimited number of thoughts. Thus one man can be not only the target of any number of opinions, affirmations, insights, inferences, and proofs but also of any number of valuations, appreciations, criticisms, eulogies, blames, reproaches, and accusations. Moreover, he can be the object of certain wishes, hopes, or fears. One can address requests, counsels, admonitions, or warnings to him; one can entertain certain intentions and purposes with regard to him, form decisions or resolutions. Finally, one can address to him certain demands, or prohibitions, or commands. In general a countless number of thoughts can descend like a swarm of flies on any object without its necessarily being affected in any way.

The difference and the relative independence of the objects from the thoughts is also shown by the fact that thoughts which refer to an object can change without any need for the object to undergo any change. Thus one can arrive at different opinions about the worth of a man without his having changed in any way actually or even in our opinion. On the other hand, the objects meant by our thoughts can change actually or in our opinion without any need that certain thoughts referring to them should change at the same time. That is, the relation of the thoughts to their objects is an "intentional" one, a mere aiming at, with no real "contact."

In addition, the objects to which the thoughts refer are always beyond the thoughts, and always transcendent to them. Even where any objects immanent in consciousness, such as one's own thinking or one's own thoughts, become the objects of new and different thoughts, these objects still are not ingredients of the thoughts referring to them but always lie beyond them. One can say, therefore, that it is part of the essential nature of thoughts to have objects beyond themselves and in this sense transcendent objects. But the pointing at objects is always immanent in the thoughts according to their essential nature.

Thus, if one pulls a single thread of thought out of the psychic life of man, it turns out that, on the one hand, it is necessarily connected with the thinking subject, whereas, on the other hand, it has just as necessarily a certain thought content through which it aims necessarily at an object. What object it is at which thinking and thought content aim in a given case depends completely upon the thought content itself. On the basis of other acts (e.g., perceptions, recollections, representations), although several objects can simultaneously stand before the eyes of the thinking subject, his thinking, through his thought content, selects this or that one in thought; only thus do these become the intended (*intentional*) objects of that thinking and those thoughts, while always remaining beyond them.

However, in the psychic life of man, thinking usually does not take place in isolation but is mostly accompanied and connected with other kinds of object consciousness and with other distinctive kinds of activities, likewise directed toward objects. Thus man, while he thinks, perceives perhaps a variety of objects. If we understand by perceiving having before oneself objects at firsthand and bodily, then this perceiving is not yet true thinking, and it is not necessarily permeated by a thinking but can be a completely unthinking look at the objects. Even if one of the objects perceived becomes an object of thinking, the thinking which refers to the object differs from the perception of the object, even though in this case it is here united with it in a special way. In a given case perception forms the basis for the thinking which refers to the perceived object. At the same time, if it is broadened and deepened to a perception of the states of affairs, it can provide the fulfilling and corroborating basis for thinking. But it is in no way the necessary presupposition for thinking, not even for the thinking of precisely those thoughts which are carried out and fulfilled on the basis of that perception. Rather, thinking can take place without any perceiving.

Regardless of how often thinking has been called a representing (*Vorstellen*) or a connecting of representations, closer consideration shows that thinking not only differs from representing but even can take place completely without any representing whatsoever, if only one understands by "representing" the genuine representing in the sense of an intuitive having-before-oneself of an object not given firsthand. It is true that an intuitive representation of the object to which thinking refers can be connected with thinking, can be its basis, and in certain cases even can form its completely adequate basis for [intuitive] fulfillment. But thinking itself is not intuitive representing; it can be performed with exactly the same thought content, even when the object to which it refers is neither intuitively represented nor at all representable. On the other hand, the merely intuitive representing is still by no means a thinking but is in itself a completely unthinking happening or a doing which is empty of thought.

Among the objects perceived or intuitively represented this one or that one can be the target of a special attention issuing from the subject. This attention flows steadily from the subject to the perceived or represented object. This attending is embedded in perceiving and representing as something special and aims at the objects. All the same, in itself it is not a thinking. If one catches oneself while attentively staring at a perceived object, one can often determine with conviction that one has in the meantime reflected about something else but has completed no thoughts at all concerning the perceived object itself—hence, that one has attended to the object without any thought. On the basis of such and similar experiences one can conceive of possible psychic beings in which all sorts of watching and attending of the most varied degree to any objects perceived or intuitively represented occur but in which any trace of thinking is absent.

It is more difficult to distinguish thinking from apperceiving for the reason that one can understand very different things by "apperceiving." However, if in connection with this word we think specifically of the mental touching, seizing, separating, combining, etc., hence of the inner manipulating of the object of perceiving and representing consciousness—a mental manipulating such as occurs often enough in the human psychic life—then we recognize that even apperceiving in this sense can occur without any thinking and is in itself a completely unthinking playing with objects of consciousness. Only when it is permeated by genuine thinking does it become a thoughtful doing.

If we now survey the total field of thinking in which we distinguished five factors, namely, the thinking subject, thinking, the thoughts, the linguistic products, and finally the objects which are affected by thinking, we see that only the thoughts are left uncovered by the other sciences. For the first two factors, the thinking subject and thinking, are already taken over by psychology as belonging to its domain. It is true that psychology cannot know thinking clearly without at the same time considering the thoughts thought in thinking. But that is no good reason why the thoughts rather than the psychic process of thinking, should be its proper subject matter.

Furthermore, the fourth factor, the linguistic products, has long been claimed by historical and systematic philology. However, this science too must direct its glance beyond the linguistic products themselves to the thoughts and elements of the thoughts expressed in them in order to know clearly and to penetrate its subject matter. But philology too deals with thoughts only secondarily, not in order to make them the center of its cognitive endeavor.

The fifth factor embraces the limitless abundance of all possible categories and areas of objects which in principle are open to thinking and thought. Of these areas all except those of thought are already distributed among the other sciences. Thus the systematic and historic natural sciences are related to material, that is, to inanimate as well as animate nature. The systematic and historical psychological sciences direct their cognitive effort to the psychic world. The world of social products and processes is encompassed by the historic and systematic social sciences. Now the area of cultural products and processes contains, among other systems, those of accumulated thought products, such as the sciences themselves and legal statutes. However, only insofar as these are historical products are they explored by certain historical sciences, such as the history of the sciences and of law. The remaining products of the cultural world are, however, occupied in their entirety by the historic and systematic cultural studies. Finally, the religious world is covered by theology.

In the area of the timeless (*irreale*) objects in which thoughts also belong, the mathematical products, in particular the magnitudes, the shapes, the geometric configurations as well as the numbers, the sets, and systems, have been appropriated by the mathematical sciences.

Hence, the world of thoughts is left as the sole still unoccupied area of objects in which a systematic science can settle down. But at once the question arises whether a systematic science of thoughts is at all possible. Aren't thoughts the field of complete arbitrariness, in which there are no barriers for the subjective preferences of thinking man? And is it possible to achieve here more than an empirical survey of the forms of webs in which man generally spins out his thoughts? Or does the world of thoughts, even if it is produced by man freely and arbitrarily, nevertheless constitute a world of forms with stable properties, with a definite order of structure and connections? Let us consider briefly, insofar as it is possible without previous detailed knowledge of the field, whether the conditions for the possibility of a systematic science with regard to the world of thoughts are fulfilled.

First, it is certain that the world of thoughts displays a great variety of firmly established kinds of thought products. A quick enumeration of a few such species will make this sufficiently clear. That there are questions, surmises, assumptions, and hypotheses; that opinions, views, judgments, assertions, theses, as well as cognitions, pieces of knowledge, insights, and truths are definitive products of thought; that in conclusions, derivations, proofs, and arguments thoughts occur in definite combinations—all this can be easily established. Furthermore, we find in stories, reports, communications,

certificates, attestations, announcements, likewise in expositions, discussions, treatises, speeches, and lectures, thought products and
thought connections of the most variegated kinds.

We encounter another group of thoughts in the estimates, evaluations, opinions, appraisals, reviews, critiques, and testimonials. Closely
related to these are the eulogies, defenses, censures, reproaches, accusations, suspicions, cursings, and condemnations.

Then enter the hopes, wishes, apprehensions, thanks, recommen-
dations, and advertisements. What also demands attention are the
various kinds of requests, counsels, warnings, admonitions, permissions, promises, and invitations.

Furthermore, in the area of voluntary enactments, the thought
products of intentions, intents, resolutions, declarations of intention,
proposals, applications, decrees, projects, and plans present themselves.
And finally the great group of thought products with an imperative
character demand notice, among which we may distinguish appeals,
summonses, ordinances, prescriptions, injunctions, commands, prohibitions, and laws.

If we face this thought world from a sufficient inner distance, so
that we can survey the whole abundance of the products which it
contains, we can easily determine that there are everywhere longer
or shorter, simpler and more complicated thoughts. Then we see
among them clear and well-ordered or more or less unclear and confused products. But what is more important for a science of thoughts
is the realization that among the thoughts there are complete, finished,
whole, and uncrippled and, on the other hand, incomplete, unfinished,
half-done, and crippled thoughts. For this points to a definite order
under which definite thoughts must contain a definite number of
elements in a definite arrangement if they are to be complete thoughts.

If we realize in addition that besides the meaningful thoughts
there are also meaningless or senseless thoughts, a specific lawful
order is revealed inasmuch as only specific elements of thought in a
specific arrangement can yield meaningful thoughts. Moreover, we see
that certain thoughts, because they have precisely this definite inner
composition, are necessarily charged with an inner contradiction,
whereas others, on the basis of their different composition, are intrin-
sically free from contradiction. If then we also pay attention to the
connections of thoughts, the remarkable and logically important fact
appears that thoughts, regardless of whether they have been put into
connection by any thinking beings, are either in connection or completely without connection and that some thoughts are in direct contradiction to each other. Special emphasis is also in order with regard
to the connections of validity and entailment, which are likewise

completely independent of whether any thinking subject puts definite thoughts into a connection of validity or entailment. These connections are the reason for the fact that the validity of specific thoughts necessarily entails the validity of other specific thoughts and that the justification of specific thoughts can be demonstrated only by quite specific other thoughts. This is true of all kinds of thoughts. After all, even in everyday life for all thoughts we distinguish between logical and illogical thoughts and connections of thoughts. Indeed, one cannot only judge and infer logically and illogically but can also ask, request, advise, wish, hope, fear, will, and give orders logically and illogically.

Besides, thoughts and connections of thoughts also show *aesthetic* differences. Some are delicate and elegant, others crudely and clumsily constructed. There are thoughts which are shaped more or less beautifully or more or less hideously. Just have a look at some thought products of Schopenhauer and Kant. Finally, quite a few thoughts, through their structure and their connection, yield very definite kinds of thought styles, which are relatively independent of their linguistic style. Even in the area of thoughts there is a baroque style, a rococo style, a Biedermeier style, and a Gothic style.

On this basis it is probable that the world of thoughts fulfills the objective conditions necessary for a systematic science. It should be easy to see that the subjective conditions can be fulfilled in order to achieve a systematic science of the thoughts. Man indeed can isolate and fixate the thoughts he thinks. They are accessible to his seizing and thinking. He then can compare several thoughts with each other, distinguish them, separate from them what they have in common; besides, he can dissect them, take away something from them, add something to them, vary something in them; finally, he can put together several of them and recognize their relations and connections; in short, in relation to the thoughts he can perform all those acts which necessarily must be performed in order for us to obtain a systematic science of them. To be sure he must think the thoughts in a different manner from the one in which they are usually thought.

For there are three different ways in which thoughts and judgments can be thought. The first is the naïve expressionist way in which man usually thinks his thoughts. It is characterized by the fact that in exclusive concentration on the objects of his thinking man forms his thoughts but does not pay any attention to the ones he has formed. Even when he formulates his thoughts by language, he dismisses them, as it were, unnoticed in their linguistic garb. At most his attention runs behind them without recapturing and receiving them back. To man the unconsidered and uncritical random thinking and talking, this naïve way of mere self-expression, is at first the natural thing. The consequence is that even immediately afterward he no longer quite knows what he has thought and said. But it would be mistaken to assert in such cases that his thinking and speaking occurs "unconsciously." Man is well aware of this thinking and speaking; in fact, he is conscious to a very high degree even of the thoughts he thinks and the speech sounds he produces. But as they escape him at the same time, he does not hold on to them as finished products and does not arrest them for a prolonged stay before his inner eye.

Now it is precisely the latter thing which is added in the second way of thinking and expressing thoughts, the critically exploring way of thinking. True, even here, as the thoughts are produced in their linguistic garb, the main concentration is focused on the objects of the thoughts, but at the same time a lateral arm of attention is turned back on the produced and linguistically clothed thoughts, receives them back through the linguistic clothing, and examines them as to their adequate linguistic formulation and their objective truth. Finally, even during the producing and linguistic formulating of the thoughts, the critically exploring lateral glance is directed to the created products in their state of being born (*status nascendi*), as it were. With this the stage of considered and critical thinking of thoughts has been reached. But at this stage too neither the thoughts themselves nor their linguistic expression is the main subject matter of consideration. Even here the objects to which the thinking and the thoughts refer are still in the center. Nevertheless, the backward-directed glance can turn more toward the linguistic formulation—if linguistic accuracy or beauty is to be aimed at—or more toward the thoughts themselves, if the refinement and the style of these thoughts are important.

Only when during the thinking of thoughts the center of gravity of attention is removed from the objects of the thinking—in which case, however, we must not lose these objects completely from our sight or the thoughts will dissolve—and only when in listening back the center of gravity is shifted to the thoughts themselves, has the stage of logical thinking proper been reached. This logical thinking usually is not supported by the necessary lateral attention to the objects of thought but at the same time holds fast to the linguistic expressions; however, it must not be chained to them but must move on to the rarefied and dark atmosphere of the thoughts themselves in order to settle down there and abide.

These different ways of thinking thoughts do not change anything in the content of the thoughts. It is rather that the same thought can be thought in these different manners. Only in naïve expressionist thinking will the thought often escape the unaccustomed backward grasp completely or in part and at times leave in its hands merely an empty linguistic garment. However, practice will insure the catch to the logical grasp backwards and by stripping off the linguistic forms present the thought body unharmed. This logical grasp backwards for seizing the thoughts that are thought will not necessarily rush after the thinking of the thoughts in temporal succession but will eventually be able to accompany the thinking of the thoughts from the start in wakeful superposition and to be present at the very birth of the thoughts.

To be sure, for a logical investigation a second thinking must be built on top of all this, without dissipation of the first. Acts of comparison, distinction, seizing of the common and the different, dissections, removal and addition of elements—the last, of course, with simultaneous initiation of the underpinning acts—must take place in order to arrive, via the mere logical intuiting of the thoughts, at insights about them. The difficulty of the logical grasp backwards, the unaccustomed manipulation of the fine thin threads of the thought webs, makes logical thinking and exploring for most people an exceedingly tiring and sterile activity which they confront with timid respect but at the same time with hateful disparagement.

Still other ways of thinking thoughts can be identified, but they are less relevant to logic. Thus, for example, the thoughts of other people can be absorbed and thought through linguistic communication without one's identifying with them, in that one shares the thinking of the judgments without at the same time judging spontaneously in the same or opposite sense. Or one thinks "in thought" what someone else might say and what one would answer in reply. However, for logic only thoughts as such are relevant, regardless of the way in which they are thought.

But thinking includes not only the performing of simple thoughts but also concluding or deducing. And this too can occur in very different ways, namely, in analogy to those given above, in naïve or in critically exploring investigation of the object, or in reflective-logical investigation of the thoughts. Likewise still other ways of the thinking performance of conclusions and deductions can be identified. But since even conclusions or deductions as peculiar connections of thoughts remain unaffected in their essence by all these special ways of their being performed in thinking, the logic of conclusions can disregard completely the investigation of the way in which they are performed thinkingly. Of course, the logician must carry out a definite way of performing them, but he merely has to carry them out, not make them the object of his investigation.

The possibility of making thoughts independently the subject matter of a science is based first on the fact that the *thoughts are different from thinking.* Whereas thinking is a real, temporal process which in each case concerns only a single thinking subject, thoughts are not real, temporal processes, but are per se timeless (*ideell*) products. Whatever can be said rightly about thoughts, namely, that they can be formulated in language, pronounced, communicated, presented, laid down, written down, collected, and ordered, makes no real sense with regard to thinking. One cannot lay down thinking, collect it, and order it. Likewise, one can absorb, explain to oneself, think through, examine, understand, and appropriate thoughts but not thinking. Also, thinking cannot be supported by reasons, proved, or refuted, but one can very well support thoughts by reason, prove, or refute them.

Besides, the difference of thoughts from thinking is borne out by the fact that in the disconnected thinking of one and the same individual, and also in that of different individuals, thoughts can be thought which are in close connection, while conversely in connected thinking completely disconnected thoughts can be thought. It is, therefore, not surprising that a contradiction between thoughts can occur without conflict of the thinking in which they are thought. "Two souls and one thought," i.e., one and the same thought, thought in numerically and qualitatively different styles of thought by different thinking subjects, would be quite impossible if thoughts were not different from thinking.

Thoughts are also by no means real components of thinking. Surely thoughts occur in thinking and only in thinking. But it does not follow from this at all that they are psychic and real components of that thinking in which they "occur." Rather, the relation between thinking and the thoughts is a very peculiar one. Language conceives of it as a relation of production by allowing us to say that the thoughts are formed, spun out, brought forth, or produced by thinking. But this producing still is not a forming of the thoughts from a found material, as is assumed by the theory which asserts that concepts are obtained from the perceived objects by the abstracting, combining, and separating of the parts, elements, and factors of objects. In this way what one gets, again and again, are only objects and no concepts, just as one cannot obtain thoughts from the repeated combination of the objects thus obtained. Concepts and thoughts are not made from object-stuff but consist of a stuff *sui generis,* as it were.

Accordingly, it also definitely would not be right to take [the phrase] "spinning out thoughts" literally and to think that the thinking subject, comparable to a spider, by secreting a psychic stuff spins forth the thoughts from this same stuff. For if we understand by this thought-stuff not the objects to which the thoughts refer but the "what," the essential stuff of which the thoughts consist, we must assert the view that the thoughts consist of a "stuff" essentially different from thinking. By spinning out thoughts, thinking does not discharge anything that is of the same kind or merely a transformed thinking, as it were, but it transcends the sphere of psychic and of all other reality and creates something purely timeless (*ideell*). If one, therefore, remains in the psychological attitude, hence if one is directed exclusively toward the grasping of what is psychically real, one will find no thoughts at all and in principle will be unable to find them.

Also, thoughts are definitely not contained in thinking as the general is in the particular or individual. Thoughts are not species or genera of thinking. If one understands by "ideating abstraction" (Husserl) the grasping of species and genera "in" the individual, then it is impossible to gain thoughts through an ideating abstraction directed toward the individual, real thinking. Rather, in this way one would never arrive at anything but certain species or genera of thinking, that psychic activity. Hence, no *psychological* observation or knowledge will ever be able to discover thoughts.

If we want to continue designating thoughts as products of thinking, hence to look at the relation between thinking and thoughts as one of production, we must emphasize at the same time that this relation of production is an absolutely unique one which must not be identified with any other relationship of the kind but must be acknowledged untouched in its unique individuality.

A systematic science of thoughts will, therefore, with regard to these peculiar thought products, have the task of finding out the essential nature and the kinds of thought; of isolating the ultimate elements out of which they are built; of exploring the kinds and the laws of the structure of the different kinds of thought; and of investigating the various conditions, relations, and connections in which thoughts of the same and different kinds stand to each other.

To be sure, two different points of view for the exploration of the world of thought emerge at once. One can forego any consideration of the aesthetic value qualities and the various styles of the thought and investigate the thoughts purely theoretically. Or one can focus specifically on the value qualities and the styles of the thoughts and investigate how these are based on the various forms and connections among the thoughts. In this case one aims at the development of an *aesthetics* and a theory of style of thoughts. However, in the former case one aspires to a purely theoretical science of the thoughts. Let our consideration in what follows be devoted solely to this theoretical science.

Summary: If, therefore, one abandons the naïve-expressionist kind of thinking; if one ceases to concentrate exclusively on the objects of thinking and to produce and express thoughts in language only casually without special notice; if then one goes beyond even the critically exploring thinking of the researcher who has split off a side arm of his attention directed toward the objects and has turned it back to his thoughts about the objects; if, thus, one turns the main arm of attention completely back to the thoughts as thought, yet without losing sight completely of the objects to which the thoughts refer; then that peculiar world opens up which forms the possible subject matter of a special science, i.e., of a systematic theory of thought. We know from daily life that in this idea-like sphere there are variegated products of thought labelled with different names, which, though produced by human thinking, show a proper being and a stubborn law of their own by which, once they are produced, they confront thinking man with their demands.

It, therefore, is to be surmised that they fulfill the objective conditions of a science. Besides, we know that with regard to these thought products we can carry out the subjective activities of comparing, distinguishing, abstracting, dissecting, removing, adding, changing components, and, furthermore, the activities of combining and separating several thought products, activities which are necessary in order to fulfill subjectively the conditions for a science of the idea-like sphere to come into being. The bending back of the glance which is needed to make the thought products become visible by themselves is, however, an unaccustomed achievement, hence difficult to maintain, and the glance remains so much glued to the brighter objects, the linguistic forms, and the psychic process of thinking that to the unaccustomed eye the place of the thought products appears rather dark and empty—something is present, but at first nothing specific can be recognized. Only with increasing practice and adaptation to this artificial focusing does this place fill up more and more distinctly.

Thus not only is this territory of thoughts, still unoccupied by the other sciences, the subject matter of a possible science, but it *must* be investigated by theoretical man as a knower if he wants to do justice to his own essence. For it is part of man's fundamental nature (*Grundwesen*) that by thinking he ought to take possession of everything that can be known at all. The light of his knowledge, therefore, must turn backwards even upon this unoccupied territory by way of reflection and elucidation.

[II] TRADITIONAL LOGIC

IF AFTER THIS PREVIEW of a systematic science of thoughts we take a look at logic as it actually appears in the history of philosophy, we find that, in spite of differences in detail, it always has had concepts, judgments, and inferences as its subject matter. It may be that at one time the inferences are in the foreground of consideration, while the judgments are studied only as components of the inferences and the concepts are studied as the components of the judgments; at another time perhaps the judgments are in the center while the concepts are considered as components of the judgments and the inferences are viewed as specific connections of judgments. Nevertheless, it is always the concepts, the judgments, and the inferences which make up the staple of all logic that has appeared thus far.

Now judgments are nothing but a special kind of thoughts, namely, thoughts which assert something. Judgments are products of thinking and are, therefore, the thought content of definite acts of thinking which is expressed in definite linguistic statements. Judgments are necessarily related to objects about which they assert something. In short, they are precisely in the place where thought products are located in the context of that thinking of thinking beings which is related to objects and expressed in definite linguistic forms. However, the concepts, as distinguished from the words in language, are nothing but the thought elements of which judgments and all other thoughts consist. Finally, on closer inspection inferences turn out to be thought combinations of a definite kind, namely, those in which from one or more judgments another judgment is inferred. Therefore, logic up to now has actually always been a theoretical science of thoughts. However, it has included in its compass the asserting thoughts exclusively—hence, neither questions, assumptions, surmises, and the like, nor those other thoughts which we call evaluations, critiques, appraisals, requests, counsels, admonitions, warnings, resolutions, intents, prescriptions, commandments, prohibitions, orders, or laws. So indeed logic is *not* a theory of thinking as a psychic process but is always a definite part of a systematic science of thoughts. But there is no recognizable reason in the nature of things why logic should confine itself forever to the special class of asserting thoughts, their elements, and their connections. Therefore, in the future logic necessarily will expand over the entire area of thoughts and have to coincide with the systematic science of thoughts characterized above. For the time being we must distinguish the traditional logic as logic in the narrower sense from the logic in the larger sense which comprises *all* kinds of thought.

Logic as a science, like all other sciences, is itself a system of thoughts. But in contrast to the other sciences it has thoughts as the subject matter of its knowledge. Now one cannot have thoughts apart from thinking. In order to focus on the subject matter of logic, one, therefore, has to carry out definite thinking and at the same time bend the glance back to the thoughts which have been thought and keep them fixated. But then a second thinking must be added which refers to the thoughts thought and fixated in the first thinking and takes them as the guiding model for the formation of a second stratum of thought. This double thinking, necessary for logical knowledge and built up in stages, constitutes the special difficulty present in logical investigations, a difficulty which can be overcome only by persistent practice. As stated before, one is always in danger of being diverted from the thoughts to the objects or the linguistic forms and of making statements about them, rather than about the thoughts.

[III] PSYCHOLOGISM

BY DEFINING LOGIC as the systematic science of thoughts we are relieved of the border conflict with psychology. Let us devote only a few words to so-called psychologism. In general, psychologism pertains not only to logic and the logical objects but also comprises ethics and aesthetics and the aesthetic and ethical objects. Let us consider here only psychologism in logic. Incidentally, everything that has to be said can easily be extended to aesthetics and ethics.

Usually psychologism contains two essentially different though connected assertions in indiscriminate confusion. The first of these assertions is to the effect that the subject matter of logic *is* something psychic. Both thinking and thoughts are nothing but certain occurrences in the psychic life of man. Hence, a scientific investigation of this subject is nothing but a part of psychology, and logic, therefore, can be nothing but a psychology of thinking, or, if one prefers, a psychology of thoughts. We owe the definitive refutation of psychologism in this sense to Edmund Husserl, who in the first volume of his *Logische Untersuchungen* has demonstrated that logic, by its peculiar subject matter as well as by its methods and its results, differs very essentially from psychology. Reference is made here to that work.

The erroneous identification of logic with the psychology of thinking has its basis in the blindness to everything timeless (*Ideelles*), in the exclusive openness for realities which leads to a confusion and interchange of thoughts with thinking. But once the essential difference between thinking and thoughts has been recognized, once it has been understood that thoughts, although they are a product of creative thinking and only occur in real thinking, differ essentially from thinking as a real psychic process, psychologism still can be advocated in [the form of] that second assertion which it usually comprises mixed with the first. In this second assertion it is expressly admitted that thoughts are well-distinguished from the thinking in which they are thought and that logic, therefore, differs in its subject matter from the psychology of thinking. But then it is added that the logical insights into thoughts lacked sufficient foundation until they were supported by corresponding psychological insights into thinking, so that logic all along the line has had to be supported by the psychology of thinking. For some people the argument upon which these psychologistic assertions are based is very seductive. This argument, therefore, will be examined here in brief summary.

Thoughts, so runs this argument, are completely dependent structures which exist merely by the grace of the thinking which produces them and are in themselves something without essence, without matter, without a being of their own. Like their being, their properties, their mutual differences, and their connections stem completely from the thinking of man. Whatever can be rightly asserted of them is the case merely because human thinking is as it is. Thus thoughts have neither a being of their own nor laws of their own, but in both respects they merely participate in the being and laws of human thinking. This is manifest even concretely if one investigates definite logical insights in detail as to their sufficient reasons. For instance, the fact that two mutually contradictory judgments cannot both be true, as the logical law of contradiction asserts, has its foundation in the fact, to be established psychologically, that man is unable to consider both these judgments as true. Likewise, the logical insight that definite thought elements, for example, a subject concept, are necessary parts of a complete independent thought has its sufficient reason only in the fact that man cannot possibly perform a complete thought without such thought elements, that is, without a subject concept. The fact that only thoughts of a definite specification are meaningful, while others are necessarily meaningless, has its ground in the fact that man is able to connect a meaning with the former but no sense at all with the latter. As in these special cases, everywhere logical insight is based on psychological findings. The very method by which one establishes the truth of logical propositions, we are told, indicates this. If you want to know whether the law of contradiction is valid, try first the psychological experiment of considering two mutually contradictory judgments to be both true. Notice that this experiment, no matter how often performed, fails despite all the mobilized effort of one's thinking, so that in your own person, at least, you cannot possibly consider two contradictory judgments to be simultaneously true, whatever specific content they may have. Then proceed to make the same experiment with other people; let them try repeatedly on request to hold any two mutually contradictory judgments both to be true. Take account of the fact that without exception, at least as long as you consult sane and sufficiently adult people suited for psychological experiments, all find it impossible to consider mutually contradictory judgments to be both true at the same time. Only then, after such a psychological examination of human thinking (but now with a sufficient basis of knowledge), can and may you legitimately consider the logical principle of contradiction as really valid.

Now in order to uncover the confusion which is at the bottom of such and similar psychologistic assertions, it is necessary to keep firmly in mind what it is that is to be supported by psychological reasons; which means that we must leave unchanged the specific meaning and character of the logical propositions whose supposed psychological reasons are under consideration. Thus it must be noted that, for instance, the logical principle of contradiction refers to definite kinds of thoughts—to mutually contradictory judgments and by no means to human thinking. However, the psychological propositions do refer [primarily] to human thinking and only secondarily to the thoughts thought by the thinking. But now no valid conclusions carry over from the psychological propositions about human thinking across to the logical principle of contradiction among judgments. For from the statement that one or several or all people cannot hold two judgments simultaneously to be true, *nothing at all* follows as to the *truth* of the two judgments, nor does it follow that they cannot both be true together. As little as it follows from psychological findings that a certain percentage of people, and perhaps even mentally sick people, actually can hold such mutually contradictory judgments to be true simultaneously would it follow that an equal percentage of two mutually contradictory judgments could both be true. This insight is based on the fact that the truth of judgments is completely independent of the question as to whether or not one or several or all people consider them true. It would be possible in principle, rather, that a certain judgment could be true and could remain invariably true in spite of the fact that all or most people considered it false or at least could not consider it true. Hence, a serious examination of truth has never tried to decide the truth of a judgment by taking a poll, i.e., by asking as many people as possible by psychological examination whether they could consider that judgment as true. After all, the principle according to which a supposedly psychological proof of the principle of contradiction would have to proceed, namely, that whatever man cannot *consider* true is for this reason not actually true, is completely invalid.

But not only is the logical connection between the psychological insights and the logical propositions lacking, but the psychological propositions have not even enough carrying power to give the logical propositions sufficient support. For what is supported can never claim a greater certainty than the ground has upon which it is erected. Now the psychological findings which matter here never have an absolute certainty because the possibility is always left open that there are people who can consider true what those examined thus far could not consider true. (Let us disregard here that we have no right simply to declare insane those people who can consider mutually contradictory judgments as both true and have no right to ignore them in the psychological result. Perhaps this is justified merely if one presupposes the validity of the principle of contradiction in its independence of all psychology and makes it one criterion of mental illness.) Logical propositions according to their essential nature claim absolute certainty which cannot be shaken by any future experiences. But this claim can never be justified by psychological reasons. Thus these untouched logical propositions cannot be grounded in any way on psychological findings, since neither can the ground support them nor is the supporting connection convincing.

However, the fact that the logical propositions are not capable of psychological support is not a circumstance to be bemoaned, but it is completely indifferent, since logical propositions are not at all in need of psychological support. Rather can their truth be understood and demonstrated with finality without in the least considering human thinking and without resorting to any psychological insights about human thinking. Thus, for instance, the truth of the principle of contradiction, as will appear later in more detail, can be recognized sufficiently and insightfully solely from the nature of the mutually contradictory judgments, from the nature of truth, and from the connection of the states of affairs posited by the two judgments. In logic the consideration of the insights of other people has no other significance than in any other sciences, and it does not constitute a psychological support of the logical insights any more than it supplies a psychological confirmation of the results in the other sciences, for instance, in physics or physiology.

The fundamental mistake on which the erroneous attempt of a psychological support of the logical propositions rests consists generally in confusing the felt compulsion of thinking with the insightful necessity of being and essence (*So-sein*).

Thus on closer inspection logic turns out to be completely independent of psychology. Psychology, however, presupposes logic, as is not to be shown here in detail, in a twofold respect: like all sciences it presupposes necessarily the validity of the logical propositions, specifically that of the principle of contradiction—for instance, by declaring all the assertions which contradict its results as false; and, secondly, it must call in the knowledge of logical principles if it wants to know thinking processes in the psychic life of man with full adequacy.

Thus logic is not the theory of *thinking* but the science of *thoughts*, specifically of the asserting thoughts. Its task is to know the essential nature of thoughts, their ultimate elements, their structure, the different kinds of thoughts, and the connections and relations of the thoughts to each other. It is, therefore, neither a part of psychology nor does it need psychology for its foundation. It is a science completely independent of psychology.

Logic is not a practical science; for it says neither what one is to do or make nor how one can do it or make it, but it provides knowledge of that peculiar unique world of thoughts. It is thus a theoretical science of thoughts.

Logic is also not a normative science in the sense of a collection of commandments and prohibitions; it is not a system of imperatives. Nor is it a normative science in the sense of a presentation of ideals. Only if norms are understood not as commands or ideals but as yardsticks of judgment or evaluation, can logic rightly be called a science of norms; for its results indeed can serve for the evaluation of thoughts and the connections of thoughts. But this does not determine the character of logic itself, which all the same remains a "science of facts," though one of thought-facts. As in the case of all other sciences, it is extraneous to logic that it or its results can be used as normative yardsticks.

[IV] LOGIC AND THEORY OF KNOWLEDGE

LOGIC IS FREQUENTLY CONFUSED with the theory of knowledge, or at least combined with it. Especially toward the end of the nineteenth century there was great lack of clarity about the relation of logic to the theory of knowledge. However, logic differs from the theory of knowledge not only in its capacity as a general theory of thought but also in its traditional form, namely, as a science of judgments, concepts, and inferences. The difference ensues from the following brief consideration. The theory of knowledge is admittedly the science of knowledge. Its task is to explore the essential nature of knowledge, its elements and structure, its different kinds, its ultimate sufficient foundations, its methods, and its limits. Now knowledge, especially scientific knowledge, consists of judgments. But not every judgment is already a piece of knowledge. Instead, judgments are real instances of knowledge only if they are not only true but also if their truth is evident or demonstrated. Whoever has passed a judgment which happens to be true has not yet achieved a piece of knowledge by it until he has made evident the truth of this judgment. In the last resort the truth of a judgment can be made evident only by bringing up to the judgment itself the behavior of the objects meant by the judgment. Therefore, a study of knowledge will have to consider the judgments of knowledge not by themselves but only in relation to the behavior of the things meant by them. Logic, however, fixes its eyes on the judgments purely by themselves, without measuring them in any way against the existing states of affairs with which they mean to agree. Thus the theory of knowledge must enlarge its scope beyond logic by moving into the center of its considerations the relation of the judgments to the objects meant and to their own behavior. In order to achieve this it has to turn to the objects of knowledge themselves, independently of the judgments which refer to them.

Then it has before it, on the one hand, the judgments with a definite content of meaning and a definite claim to truth and, on the other hand, the objects themselves and their capacity to fulfill more or less perfectly by their behavior the definite claims to truth of the judgments.

In order to be able to turn to the objects of knowledge themselves, the theory of knowledge must abandon the standpoint of logic and adopt a wholly different one. For from the standpoint of logic, which is firmly anchored in the sphere of thoughts, the objects are accessible only as the supposed materials of the thoughts posited and aimed at in thought, not as they may be in and by themselves. It, therefore, is necessary to step back out of the sphere of thoughts and meanings and enter the sphere in which the objects meant present themselves on their own in firsthand authenticity, in order to be able to know how they relate themselves to the claims of the thoughts which are directed to them and in what way and to what degree they are capable of making the truth and correctness of the thoughts evident. From this epistemological standpoint thoughts are seen not as they were from the logical standpoint, from inside, as it were, and in their central axis but as if from the outside and laterally.

Since the theory of knowledge, in order to be able to fulfill its task completely from its position, requires the intrinsic clarification of the judgments, their elements, their claims to truth, their kinds and connections, and since that clarification cannot be obtained from its standpoint but can be expected only from logic, it follows that the theory of knowledge presupposes logic. However, logic can fulfill its task fully and completely without in any way presupposing or enlisting the theory of knowledge. Therefore, it not only differs from the theory of knowledge but is also completely independent of it. It is easy to see that logic, as soon as the epistemological viewpoint in it becomes predominant, must succumb to the danger of going astray, since it then can maintain its uniform standpoint only with difficulty and is easily misled to an untidy medley of logical and epistemological tasks.

Accordingly, in what follows logic is to be treated independently of any theory of knowledge and without any admixture of an epistemological investigation.

Of late, phenomenology steps forward as the fundamental philosophical science. It is not identical with the theory of knowledge but claims to precede it as its foundation. But neither is it identical with logic. In order to clarify the relation between these philosophical sciences, let us enter briefly into the relation of logic to phenomenology.

[V] LOGIC AND PHENOMENOLOGY

TO SAY BRIEFLY and yet intelligibly what phenomenology is and intends is something desired by many but at this time hardly possible. All that can be in question here is to give a certain intimation of the subject matter and the task of phenomenology and to characterize the position of logic with respect to it. Let us begin by picturing the situation which we surveyed when we analyzed the total content of thinking. The thinking subject from whom the whole variety of thought-forming acts of thinking proceeds, aiming his sights at a completely unlimited variety of objects in all possible fields of objects, develops, as these objects confront him now in this, now in that, kind of consciousness, successively with respect to the objects comprised in the surrounding world, the whole abundance of thought products of various kinds, as we have partly enumerated them above. Phenomenology shifts the point of sight of its investigation first into the thinking subject and focuses from this place on the objects within the object world of this thinking subject; it then takes hold of the thoughts and the opinions which the thinking subject harbors about the object and, in so doing, refrains from taking any stand with regard to these opinions, while taking the objects and the object worlds merely as the counterparts (seen thus or so by the subject) of his thinking consciousness, without allowing itself any [claims to] transcendent knowledge of these objects. For only from the point of sight of that thinking subject and only as intentional counterparts of that consciousness are these objects visible to it from its standpoint. Phenomenology, therefore, also leaves aside all knowledge obtained elsewhere and all the sciences of these objects, because it places itself in thought before the beginning of all such science. From the point of sight moved into the thinking subject it looks first at the intentional objects and the opinions of that subject, particularly at the acts of consciousness which pertain to these objects and opinions, and next to the modes of givenness of the objects and the modes of thought of the opinions. Indeed, even the subject into which it transfers its point of sight is left behind unheeded. Viewing in this manner it takes inventory first of what there is to be seen within the scope so staked out. It does not raise at all the question of the reality of what can thus be intuited, not even with regard to the acts of consciousness, but only pays attention to the what and the properties, as well as the mutual relations, of what is to be found there. The most cautious and most circumspect description of what is intuited is then followed especially by the tracing of the essential and necessary affinities in the various distinguishable strata of the whole, both between the elements of the same stratum and between the elements of different strata. In particular, the way in which certain elements or complexes stand in relation to certain others as their ultimate fulfillment and foundation is pursued in detail and by cautious probing. Thus phenomenology passes constantly through the different spheres: namely, those of the acts of thinking, the consciousness of objects, the opinions, and the intentional objects.

Logic, by contrast, has a much more restricted field. It stays exclusively within the sphere of thought products. But that does not make it a part of phenomenology. It investigates the thought products not only by themselves but also merely for their own sake, whereas phenomenology considers the thought products merely as the idea-like content of certain acts of thought and aims at the essential relation of the acts of thinking to other acts of thinking, to the consciousness of objects, and to the intentional objects of consciousness.

Thus logic, the theory of knowledge, and phenomenology are related in such a way that the theory of knowledge leads back on one side to phenomenology and on the other side to logic. For as the theory of knowledge undertakes to explore the ultimate foundations of all knowledge by examining both the cognition of being and the cognition of values and oughtness as to their ultimate foundations, it is led back necessarily to the supposed perceptions of being, of values, and of oughtness. But in so doing it must soon realize that there are very different kinds and modifications of such perceptions and that evidently not all have the same value in supporting knowledge. Then the theory of knowledge is forced to certain preliminary investigations about the different kinds and modifications of perception in order to determine those kinds and modifications which alone are relevant for the ultimate support of knowledge in the different areas of being, values, and oughtness. In this way the theory of knowledge is led to problems which lie properly in the domain of phenomenology. It cannot solve these problems from its own standpoint. For its work begins only after those kinds and modifications of perception are found into which it must enter in order to have before it the supposed objects of knowledge in firsthand authenticity, without veils, and in order to be able to examine their relation to the judgments which refer to them and to their claim to truth. But in so doing it transcends the tasks of phenomenology, which after all does not have the responsibility of examining and evaluating the claims of the judgments as to their truth, their justification, and their actual chance of fulfillment.

That the theory of knowledge, on the other hand, leads back necessarily to logic has become manifest to us through the fact that the theory of knowledge, in order to fulfill its task, requires the clear knowledge of judgments, their elements, their structure, their claim to truth, their kinds, and their connections; such knowledge can be supplied only by logic.

From what has been said it can be seen how far logic too needs phenomenological supplementation. For if it is to be made clear in what relation the thoughts and specifically the judgments, the concepts, and the inferences stand to the different kinds of acts of thinking and to the intentional objects, they require the sort of investigations which are in the domain of phenomenology.

[VI] PREVIEW OF THE FOLLOWING

IN WHAT FOLLOWS, of all the special types of thought [at first] only the judgment is to be examined. Indeed, the judgment will be considered first, not because concepts are really also judgments, as has been asserted at times, but because the examination of concepts presents very special difficulties. In general, judgments can be held fast more easily and are more easily recognized in their essential nature than are concepts taken by themselves. By an inspection of the judgments the logical glance is sharpened and made steadier, so that it can grasp the concepts more easily. Besides, the closer analysis of the judgments makes certain concepts stand out clearly which otherwise would tend to escape attention and which indeed have been almost completely overlooked by logic thus far. After the theory of the judgment has been considered in the first section, the theory of the concept will follow in the second section. The new contributions to be offered will give a sense of the peculiar air and nature of the pure logical objects, which have not stood out properly in traditional logic.

In the third section the highest logical principles are to be presented in such a way that after having formed an unintelligible pile of debris for so long they will be revived by a unified interpretation.

The fourth section will conclude with the doctrine of inference, in which the beginnings of a new construction will be presented.

4 / Theory of Knowledge
and Phenomenology

THE LAST SELECTION from Pfänder's writings on phenomenology is a posthumous text. It is definitely not one which he himself would have wanted to see published during his lifetime, let alone translated. Yet it is the only suitable substitute I can think of for the book which he tried to prepare for publication: his *Introduction to Philosophy and Phenomenology*. Had it been completed it would have contained more and less than the following text: more, in that it would have been a developed conspectus of philosophy by way of consistent application of the phenomenological method; less, in that his theory of phenomenology and its relation to epistemology was to be given only incidentally in the context of his concrete discussions.

This is one of the reasons why a text such as "Theory of Knowledge and Phenomenology," which, incidentally, was kept in a separate folder among Pfänder's papers (*Pfänderiana* #36), is still unique. But it has to be read in full awareness of its condition and its limited purpose.

In 1929 Pfänder had been invited for a lecture in the *Kantgesellschaft* in Prague, where the Brentano tradition with its interest in a realistic phenomenology was going strong. It is no longer possible to establish how far this consideration was on Pfänder's mind. In any case, he used this invitation as an occasion to formulate and present systematically some of his views on the meaning and proper role of phenomenology as he had come to conceive of them. Usually, Pfänder lectured freely, without a manuscript; but for this occasion he had prepared a set of coherent notes, almost always in complete sentences, as a sort of précis of what he wanted to say. In fact, there is even a second set of such notes, written more than a month later, followed by the theses translated at the end, which overlaps with the earlier text and may be related to the subsequent discussion of the lecture.

The main significance of this text is that it contains the last explicit statement of Pfänder's conception of phenomenology in its relation to other parts of philosophy and science. It also tries to present the phenomenological approach as the only possible way of breaking the deadlock between the epistemologies of rationalism, empiricism, and Kantianism, all of which, in Pfänder's view, misinterpret the genuine meaning of knowledge and are unable to justify its claims.

This was also the first occasion on which Pfänder stated his own solution. According to it, epistemology, so often conceived of as the ultimate foundation for all claims to knowledge, presupposes phenomenology without coinciding with it. In fact, it actually has two such foundations:

(1) phenomenology as the study of the consciousness in which the supposed objects of our knowledge are presented; and

(2) a study which at times Pfänder does not yet call phenomenology in the full sense but which he considers merely a phenomenological clarification of meaning, i.e., a study which tries to determine what we really mean when we make certain claims about certain things. It is not hard to see that this first stage of phenomenology comes very close to, if it does not coincide with, the study of ordinary language.

Of course these formulations must not be considered as final. Comparing them with the way in which Pfänder applied his new method in his later works, one realizes that he had not yet fully worked out the three steps which he later distinguished, namely, (1) clarification of meaning; (2) *epoché;* and (3) perceptual verification. But the ingredients are all there. Nevertheless, this is the first explicit statement of Pfänder's version of phenomenology, which he also called the Munich phenomenology. While it begins with careful clarification of meanings and is followed by a deliberate suspension of belief in Husserl's sense, its center of gravity is the analysis of perceptual givenness, in which the various acts of perceiving, their objective correlates, and the modes of their givenness have to be cautiously explored. It is clear that in Pfänder's view such a discriminating phenomenology will also enable us to distinguish from within the veridical types of perception from their counterfeits in such a way that the foundations for a phenomenological realism can be laid. To decide whether and how far these foundations, in the undeveloped shape in which Pfänder left them, are adequate is a task which transcends the scope of the present introduction.—H. S.

AFTER DESCARTES the theory of knowledge had been considered as the ultimate and necessary foundation of philosophy. Since about 1900 phenomenology has come forward with the claim of being the ultimate foundation of the theory of knowledge, philosophy, and all the sciences. Its task is most easily revealed if we start out from the theory of knowledge and realize that it requires phenomenology as its necessary foundation.

The theory of knowledge seeks to know the essential nature, the structure, the kinds, the methods, and the limits of knowledge. Pieces of knowledge (*Erkenntnisse*) are judgments which are not only true but also manifestly true. Pieces of direct knowledge are those which are known to be true immediately; pieces of indirect knowledge are those which are known to be true indirectly, that is, from the truth of other pieces of knowledge. The latter presupposes direct knowledge. Pieces of knowledge must refer to objects. Their truth is based on their relation of adequacy to the autonomous behavior of the objects to which they refer. The truth of pieces of immediate knowledge can become manifest only if the objects and their respective autonomous behavior are manifest. The necessary presupposition and ultimate foundation of all knowledge is, therefore, the consciousness of the objects to which it refers.

The consciousness in which real objects are manifest authentically (*selbst leibhaftig*) is called experience. There is a theory of knowledge which states that all knowledge is based ultimately on experience; this theory is called "empiricism" (*Empirismus*).

However, there is a kind of knowledge which refers directly to such objects as are not given in experience, for example, mathematical knowledge and universal knowledge. The former refers to timeless (*ideelle*) objects, the latter to an unlimited number of objects of a certain kind or to several kinds of objects. To some people these pieces of knowledge are the only authentic ones. The objects to which they refer can only be thought, not experienced. Accordingly, a different theory of knowledge states that all real knowledge is based upon clear and distinct thinking. Its name is "rationalism." In opposition empiricism asserts that even these pieces of knowledge are based on experience, inasmuch as the mathematical objects and the general, i.e., the species, become consciously known through abstraction and generalization on the basis of experiences.

Now Locke, Hume, and Kant started investigating this supposed experience more closely. They thought they could establish that many objects to which pieces of knowledge refer are never given in experience, e.g., space, time, material objects, action, forces, etc., and that they cannot be obtained from experience by abstraction. Finally Kant thought he could show that the supposed experience of the real world consisted of sensations of the actually given sense data (colors, sounds, etc.), of the necessary additive intuitions (*Hinzuschauungen*) of space and time, and of the necessary additive thinking of categories, of such connective concepts as thing, causal nexus, etc. The necessary combination of sensory, additive intuition and additive thinking, Kant thought, was the ultimate foundation of knowledge. Accordingly, experience was not an experience of a world existing by itself but was merely a being presented with a world of appearances constructed involuntarily and necessarily out of sense data, forms of intuition (space and time), and categories or connective concepts (*Verbindungsbegriffe*). But this changes the meaning of knowledge and the meaning of truth and reality.

Neither empiricism nor rationalism nor critical philosophy are real solutions of the problems of knowledge. The supposed foundations of knowledge, both experience and the process of thinking the objects, require first a more thorough and unbiased investigation. Phenomenology tries to undertake this job. It has to protect itself from the start

against possible aberrations by trying to reach the proper phenomenological attitude.

To this end it has to leave in abeyance the question of whether
some of the objects of consciousness are real by themselves or merely
phenomena. It abstains from any decision on that point; it considers
merely the what of the objects and their mode of givenness. Furthermore, it must leave in abeyance all real or supposed pieces of knowledge about the objects, including knowledge about the genesis of
experience and the achievements of thinking. Accordingly, it must not
base any of its knowledge on knowledge obtained from elsewhere. In
this sense it must be completely free from presuppositions and place
itself before the beginning of all knowledge, as it were. What is it,
then, that phenomenology still has before it in the phenomenological
attitude?

(a) Consciousness, [i.e.,] the various kinds of conscious experiences
directed toward objects

(b) The ensemble of all possible objects, but merely as counterparts
of consciousness, as phenomena

(c) The views about these objects

And how has it to proceed?

(1) First, it clarifies the views about the objects by establishing
what kinds of objects are meant, what kinds of such objects
there are, what kinds of states of affairs with regard to these
objects are meant, and what kinds of such states of affairs
there are in our meanings. This in itself is not yet phenomenology, but it certainly is necessary preliminary work for it.

(2) Next, it establishes that the objects and the states of affairs
meant can be objects of consciousness in different modes.
They may be merely meant, thought, represented. But some
of them may be perceived, that is, they may be so fully conscious that they [may be considered as] given authentically
exactly as they are meant. In this case there is no sense in
trying to get still closer to them with our consciousness.

(3) It then records how those acts of consciousness are constituted,
how the objects and states of affairs themselves are given
authentically. It turns out that a special kind of conscious *acts*
with a distinctive structure corresponds to each special type
of *objects*—acts in which they are really and authentically
given.

(4) Further, it investigates whether and how far the acts of consciousness to which certain objects and states of affairs are
authentically given merely receive the objects and states of
affairs unadulterated, or whether and how far they produce

these objects as appearances, [i.e.,] whether and how far they are receptive or productive.

These investigations are to be undertaken successively in the case of all kinds of objects and states of affairs which appear authentically in specific, more or less complicated acts of consciousness. But [they are also to be performed] in the case of both the so-called "general" objects and the timeless objects. So phenomenology is the foundation of all philosophy, [but] it is not philosophy *itself* (*die Philosophie*).

It is the foundation of all sciences; [but it is] not itself all the sciences.

THESES

(1) Theory of knowledge requires phenomenology as its foundation.

(2) Phenomenology is not a mere method of philosophy which one might take or leave.

(3) It is phenomenology, and no longer the theory of knowledge, which is the necessary foundation of all philosophy. But it does not replace the theory of knowledge.

(4) Phenomenology is the philosophical science of the consciousness of objects, more specifically of the consciousness of objects in which the conscious objects appear as authentically given. To mean an object and to have it consciously are two different things.

(5) Different kinds of consciousness in which the different kinds of objects are authentically given correspond to these objects.

(6) Phenomenology has the task of determining the different kinds of objects and their structures, just as they are meant (clarification of meaning).

(7) Next, it has to find out whether and in what acts the objects meant are corporeally given.

(8) At first it must necessarily disregard reality, truth, and sciences. [It has to disregard] also the psycho-physical theory of perception (*epoché*).

Appendix A / The Idea of a Phenomenological Anthropology and Alexander Pfänder's Psychology of Man[1]

THE IMMEDIATE OBJECTIVE of the present essay is to serve as an introduction to the first English translation of selected texts from the writings of Alexander Pfänder. I want to show that his phenomenology may have particular significance today for all those who have an interest in the development of a philosophical anthropology and especially in the significance of phenomenology for this development.

But I hope that beyond such a limited purpose this essay can also stimulate a more methodical and critical approach to an area where today philosophy may have special opportunities and responsibilities.

Recently there has been a good deal of discussion not only about philosophical anthropology but also about phenomenological or existential anthropology and about the phenomenology of man. But too often the appeal of such terms stands in inverse proportion to clarity of meaning and concrete fulfillment. The idea that anthropology is vitally important and that phenomenology may have something important to contribute to it seems plausible enough. But precisely what it is that it can contribute and how and why it should be able to do so seem to be questions rarely, if ever, raised explicitly.

What I want to do therefore is to reflect first on the relation of anthropology to phenomenology. I want to show what phenomenological anthropology can mean, once the phenomenological approach is clearly understood. I also want to show that thus far the real task has hardly been touched. Finally, I want to produce some evidence for the assertion that perhaps the best fulfillment of this task can be found in enterprises which are still innocent of the label "phenomenological anthropology," such as Pfänder's phenomenological psychology of man.

1. Anthropology and Philosophical Anthropology

THE RISE, or actually the revival, of philosophical anthropology in general, as the background for a phenomenological anthropology, deserves at least passing mention, especially in the Anglo-Amer-

1. This article by Herbert Spiegelberg was first published in the *Review of Existential Psychology and Psychiatry*, V (1965), 122–36, and is reprinted with the permission of the editor.

ican setting, where anthropology is on the whole still identified with the empirical science of anthropology, a vast area of studies fascinating even for philosophers. The fact that lately this anthropology has become more interested in philosophical questions on its own is one of the encouraging signs for those interested in bridge building.

Nevertheless, the idea of a *philosophical* anthropology may still grate on the more analytical, critical, and empirical nerves of Anglo-American methodologists. Let it be admitted, then, that this idea has its main origin in the more troubled and murkier waters of continental thought. Perhaps the most symptomatic and most impressive call to such an enterprise was implied in Max Scheler's statement of 1926:

> In the approximately ten thousand years of history we are the first age in which man has become completely and unrestrictedly "problematic," in which he no longer knows what he is, but knows at the same time that he does not know it.[2]

Scheler himself died too soon to complete the philosophical anthropology he had announced. Its reconstruction from his posthumous papers remains to this day an unsolved and perhaps insoluble task. All that is available now is his lecture of 1927 on "The Place of Man in the Cosmos," with its strange dualism of blind cosmic urge and powerless spirit converging in man. Scheler might also have been the philosopher to develop a genuinely phenomenological anthropology. However, it must be realized that at this stage in his development phenomenology as such no longer played an important part in his thinking.

The challenge was reinforced by the new totalitarian doctrines, especially by the Nazi myth of man the racial being but also by the growing appeal of the Marxist view of man. Yet only a systematic and critical examination could answer such basic questions as those of the essential structure of man, his distinctive features, his place in the universe, his dignity, and his destination. A mere empirical study of the varying patterns of culture, or even of cultural universals, could not yield the answers. Such questions require a philosophical approach.

2. The Idea of a Phenomenological Anthropology

PHENOMENOLOGY, at Scheler's time the most influential movement in Germany, was the most likely taker of this challenge. In what sense and to what extent could it be expected to meet it?

In order to answer this question it might be best first to consider the peculiar powers and possible limitations of phenomenology. For I do not want to aid and abet the idea that phenomenology is the philosophical Jack-of-all-trades.

Disregarding the varieties of today's interpretations of the phenomenological approach, I shall here simply postulate three minimum requirements for any approach which has a claim to call itself phenomenological:

(1) A phenomenological approach must start from a direct exploration of the experienced phenomena as they present themselves in our consciousness, paying special attention to the way in which they

2. "Mensch und Geschichte," *Philosophische Weltanschauung* (Bonn, 1929), p. 15; trans. Oscar A. Haag in *Philosophical Perspectives* (Boston, 1958), pp. 65–93.

present themselves, without committing itself to belief or disbelief in their reality.

(2) It must attempt to grasp the essential structures of these experienced phenomena and their essential interrelations.

(3) It should also explore the constitution of these phenomena in our consciousness (constitutive phenomenology), i.e., watch the way in which these phenomena take shape in our experience as it develops.

Now what would it mean to apply such an approach to anthropology? Certainly something very different from what the author of *The Phenomenon of Man*, Pierre Teilhard de Chardin, has given us in his exciting vision of man's evolution from point Alpha to point Omega, a vision which he himself sometimes called "phenomenological." One need not disparage it in denying it the title "phenomenology" in the sense of the phenomenological method as characterized above. Instead, a phenomenology of man based on this method would have to present first a picture of man *as he experiences himself immediately*, i.e., independent of all information which he may derive from science and scientific inference, which Teilhard utilized so impressively. This would mean specifically:

(1) A descriptive study of man's consciousness of himself as man. Such a study would have to be articulated in line with the analysis of intentional consciousness after the manner of Husserl, i.e., it would have to distinguish what in his terms would be called the *intending ego*, its *intending acts*, and its *intended objects*, or if one prefers Cartesian terminology, the cogitating ego, its cogitations, and its cogitata. In the case of anthropology this would involve:

(a) a study of the human ego, with its characteristically human modifications, i.e., as an ego incarnated in a body, limited in its range of senses and in bodily strength, developing, maturing, aging, and eventually dying;

(b) a study of human experiencing, i.e., of all the functions of the ego, from sensing and perceiving to thinking, feeling, and willing in their infinite variety *as modified by the human situation*, e.g., by the limited range of stimuli to which its organs can respond, by the limitation of its memory and its imagination, etc.;

(c) the study of the human world with its human objects as experienced in a human life. For this human world too essentially belongs to man, if not as a part of him, at least as his essential habitat and as his essential counterpart. A particularly important area of this world, and in fact man's only access to it, is his own body as experienced by him. This phenomenal body must of course be distinguished from his anatomical body, as studied by the biological sciences and by physical anthropology. Only that part of this body which is given in experience is part of the phenomenal body. Also, the human world includes man's creative expressions, his language, his various cultural enterprises, and his history as he experiences them.

A peculiar case is that of the human unconscious. One might first think that the unconscious is outside the sphere of a phenomenology which focuses on conscious experience. But insofar as even the subconscious can be made conscious through more or less direct methods, it is at least a potential field for phenomenological exploration. There are hopeful beginnings in this direction.

Thus the primary range of phenomenological anthropology qua descriptive enterprise would be man and his world insofar as he directly experiences himself directly, but not further than that.

(2) Simply recording these phenomenal data is, however, not all that a phenomenological anthropology would do, particularly if it were

restricted to personal accounts of each one's own experience of himself qua man. To make such descriptions phenomenological, there would have to be at least an attempt to grasp the essential nature of these phenomena as sought by an eidetic phenomenology which attempts to separate what is essential to man from what is merely contingent to his essence.

(3) Another task of phenomenology with regard to man would be an account of the peculiar ways in which man is given to himself. To illustrate the need, one might point out that one's own body is given at best in a strangely distorted visual perspective, in which what are perhaps the most vital organs, including his sense organs and the whole back, are not given at all directly and if so only laterally in a very blurred way. The consideration of these modes is even more important in the case of the subconscious.

(4) Yet all these undertakings would deal only with the static phenomenon of man. But man is anything but a static being. His life is not only a temporal structure but is in a distinctive sense a historical one. He passes through definite stages in his development. This raises the question of the connections between these temporal phases and stages. How far are they understandable? What would such understanding mean in comparison with mere causal explanation? To give such understanding by an exploration of the concrete connections would be the concern of an interpretive phenomenology. Its goal is the kind of understanding which goes by the seemingly untranslatable German term *verstehen*. In a sense all essential insights are cases of such understanding. Under the name of "hermeneutic phenomenology," Heidegger has made a special effort to penetrate into the deeper and less obvious meanings of human existence. Man in his short-range and long-range enterprises certainly poses peculiar challenges for such an undertaking. In any event, the understanding of what can be found out about the essential motivations of human behavior is a legitimate concern of phenomenology, especially when these motives are phenomena given in direct experience.

In short, then, a phenomenological anthropology so conceived is one in which man is to be studied as he appears to himself with his human consciousness, his experienced body, and his experienced world in their historical development. Such an approach does not exclude the possibility of, and in fact the need for, complementary approaches to man in order to complete the task of a comprehensive philosophical anthropology. This philosophical anthropology would have to include the more objective information supplied by the biological sciences and other studies that must contribute to a panorama like that of Teilhard de Chardin.

What then is the peculiar significance of phenomenology in anthropology? Why should there be such a special phenomenological anthropology? Why not also, for instance, a phenomenological physics or botany? Now it is true that there are phenomenological aspects even of these fields. But phenomenology has a rather different and more central significance for the sciences of man. For *man* is a being who essentially appears to himself. And this appearance makes an essential part of his very being, perhaps his most essential part. In this sense man, the object of anthropology, is essentially a phenomenological being. He and his behavior cannot be understood without knowing how he appears to himself. There is therefore every reason to take this phenomenal aspect of man seriously. This does not mean that phenomenological anthropology should be set apart from philosophical anthropology. But it may be worth considering whether phenomenological anthropology should not eventually be handled as a special division within the comprehensive framework of philosophical anthropology, the division which would explore man's experiences of, and perspectives on, himself.

3. Phenomenological Anthropology Thus Far

To THE BEST of my knowledge there is not yet any systematic text under the title "phenomenological anthropology." Are there at least any solid preparations for one, perhaps under a different name?

As far as the philosophers are concerned, I know at least of one German book, *The Philosophische Anthropologie*, by Hans-Edward Hengstenberg (1957), originally a student of Max Scheler, which begins with a section "Concerning the Phenomenology of Man," followed by three more on the metaphysics of man dealing with his *Geist*, with human life, and with the human whole respectively. But even the part on phenomenology has little to do with the program I have outlined, concentrating as it does on the facts of human attitude such as man's capacity for objectivity (*Sachlichkeit*). So whatever may be considered as phenomenological anthropology in my sense could only be found under different labels.

Husserl, the fountainhead of the Phenomenological Movement, mentions the idea of a "phenomenology of man" (*Phänomenologie des Menschen*) in the *Ideen* as one of several phenomenologies to be undertaken after the phenomenological reduction has surrounded the natural world with the appropriate brackets, which are to deal with "his personality, his personal qualities, and his (human) flow of consciousness." [3] But he remained suspicious of all *Anthropologie* as another form of anthropologism, against which he had fought in his *Logische Untersuchungen* as a variety of psychologism, warning against it specifically in his lecture on "Phenomenology and Anthropology." [4] Yet indirectly he gave special impetus to the study of the human life-world by his late stress on the *Lebenswelt* as a particularly promising avenue to his transcendental phenomenology.

Heidegger protested vigorously against the confusion of philosophical anthropology with his existential analytics. But since he equated human *Dasein* with man himself, it was not surprising that his analyses of such conceptions as that of being-in-the world proved particularly stimulating for the later development of a philosophical anthropology based on man's appearance to himself.

Among the French, Gabriel Marcel ought to be mentioned for his new emphasis on the importance of the phenomenal body. This theme is developed further in Merleau-Ponty's *Phenomenology of Perception*, though it should be pointed out that the phenomenal body is by no means absent from the writings of such German phenomenologists as Husserl and Scheler. But all this is at best raw material for a real phenomenological anthropology.

For a more explicit formulation of this idea one has to turn to those psychiatrists who saw in phenomenology the most promising approach to a real understanding of man in his entirety, normal as well as abnormal. Ludwig Binswanger is the most prominent advocate of such

3. *Ideas* I, §76.
4. "Phänomenologie und Anthropologie," *Philosophy and Phenomenological Research*, II (1941), 1–14; trans. Richard Schmitt in *Phenomenology and the Background of Realism*, ed. R. M. Chisholm (Chicago, 1960).

an anthropology. Actually, it was he who gave the title "Concerning Phenomenological Anthropology" to the first volume of his major essays, when he republished them with an important introduction in 1947. He indicated that he had chosen this title because the method of these essays was phenomenological, "since they had resulted from his occupation with Husserl's phenomenology," and because their subject matter was the essential relations and structures in human beings. An even more impressive result of Binswanger's concern was his magnum opus of 1942 on the "Basic Forms and the Knowledge of Human *Dasein*" (*Grundformen und Erkenntnis menschlichen Daseins*). But even this work can hardly be considered a comprehensive system of phenomenological anthropology, nor does Binswanger make such a claim. For its major concern is the phenomenology of love in the sense of the loving relationships of men, culminating in "we-hood" (*Wirheit*). No other aspect of man is considered.

The situation is basically the same with regard to the otherwise very significant contributions to a phenomenological anthropology which can be found in the studies of Viktor von Gebsattel, Eugène Minkowski, Erwin Straus, and F. J. J. Buytendijk, who are closest to Binswanger in objective and approach. All of them offer phenomenological treatments of certain aspects of philosophical anthropology. None of them claims to present a fully developed system.

What in recent years has been offered in the United States as existential psychology and psychiatry, and even as anthropological phenomenology (Rollo May, Adrian van Kaam), contains a number of promising themes. But it is thus far anything but a systematic realization of the program of a phenomenological anthropology.

It seems, therefore, safe to state that to this hour the idea of a genuinely phenomenological anthropology remains a program, though by no means any longer an empty one. It is more than likely to lead to more systematic and fruitful realizations in the near future. Perhaps the greatest promise for its fulfillment is the recent work of Paul Ricoeur.

4. Pfänder and the Phenomenology of Man

To CONNECT the name of Pfänder with phenomenological anthropology may at first blush seem like an anachronism. For the term was not yet born when, around 1933, he had completed his main work in the field.[5] To attach this name to his phenomenological psychology, therefore, a generous extension of the label, making his a phenomenological anthropology *avant la lettre*, as the French would say.

Nevertheless, as far as the substance is concerned, no other phenomenological enterprise comes so close to fulfilling the specifications of my program as Pfänder's phenomenological psychology, and particularly his last work of 1933, *Die Seele des Menschen*.

Just how close Pfänder's ultimate objective in psychology and even in philosophy was to the development of a philosophical anthropology can be seen best from his own translation of an announcement of his last work, whose German original was never published.[6] It may at

5. Pfänder himself refers to the "old name 'Anthropologie' as a possible label for a study of man as a unified whole, a label which, however, had recently acquired a "somewhat different meaning." (*Die Seele des Menschen* [Halle, 1933], p. 4.) But all he promises is a psychology of man's psyche and its life.

6. See below, pp. 83–85.

the same time serve as an example of his style and, by implication, of the man.

This text may at first give the impression that Pfänder's main concern was still psychology, though it was a new psychology, one which was specifically focused on man, in this sense a humanist psychology but not yet an anthropology which would deal with more than man's psyche. However, a closer inspection will reveal that much more is involved.

To be sure, Pfänder's earlier work as a phenomenological psychologist was mainly an attempt to enlarge the horizon of traditional psychology for its own sake, which Pfänder wanted to turn away from its preoccupation with psycho-physics and physiology. He also aimed at relieving the poverty of its psychological content by a fresh phenomenological approach to the basic phenomena and by introducing new ones which had escaped even the eyes of more perceptive psychologists such as his teacher Theodor Lipps, of empathy fame. In this manner, Pfänder explored particularly the phenomena of the will, the subject of his *Phenomenology of Willing* of 1900, and added to this book in his even more influential essay of 1911 on "Motives and Motivation." A similar enrichment was his phenomenology of the sentiments (*Gesinnungen*) of 1913, showing new dimensions in such familiar phenomena as love and hatred, a study which attracted the admiration of Ortega y Gasset. Finally, in his "Fundamental Problems of Characterology" of 1924, he broke completely new ground by developing a new framework for describing the varieties of human personality.

All this descriptive work, though not yet focusing on man explicitly, showed Pfänder's intense interest in the full concreteness of human life and personality. But his supreme bid for not only encompassing but understanding man in his entirety was his last book on man's psyche. The "Author's Announcement," added at the end of this paper in translation, contains a condensed abstract of its main argument. In the present context only those features of this conception need mentioning which are pertinent to the development of a phenomenological anthropology. I shall therefore confine my report about this 400-page work to the following sketch:

Basic is the distinction between the psyche's life and the psyche itself. As far as its life is concerned, Pfänder begins with a colorful survey of its varieties in it cognitive, affective, and practical manifestations. Special attention is given to its relations with the body and with the world in which it occurs. There follows a detailed attempt to understand this life. Pfänder traces it back to a network of "drives" or fundamental tendencies, e.g., toward having or avoiding, toward achieving, toward acting, toward power, etc. These in turn are derived from an original drive toward the creative unfolding of man's general and individual fundamental essence, with the essential cooperation of the active ego. This essence can be discerned by means of a peculiar theoretical idealization based on empirical observation. The essential structure of the human psyche thus revealed is that of a living being, directed toward a world, with an organized psychic structure, with a body, a being which is reflective, personal, i.e., controlled by an ego, ethical, social, and even religious. Psyches differ in volume, configuration, texture, etc. Eventually Pfänder tries to show that the psyche is a meaningful and understandable unit, understandable as tending toward the unfolding of these essential characteristics in the context of its world.

In what sense and to what extent can such an anthropology be claimed as phenomenological anthropology?

The first doubt may easily be: Does it really deal with man as a whole? It may deal with his psyche. But what about his body? Now this doubt would be well taken if we were concerned with the task of a comprehensive *philosophical* anthropology, which must of course take account of man's full bodily structure. And it is true that Pfänder deliberately ignores anatomy and physiology in the study of man's real body. But all the more does he deal with the *phenomenal* body, as it is experienced in the life of the psyche. In fact, Pfänder gives the body a much more important place in the psyche's economy than is done in most other psychologies and even phenomenologies. Thus he sees in the body neither the mere physical basis for the existence of the psyche nor the mere vantage point from which we perceive objects in space, as often seems to be the case in Husserl. For Pfänder the body is also the mediator between the psyche and the world and its fitting representative in and to it. What Pfänder has to say on this point and on the bodily, as distinguished from the psychic, drives belongs to the most original and colorful parts of his work. This is phenomenology of the body at its best and qualifies his psychology as a piece of phenomenological anthropology, if not yet as a philosophical anthropology.

In passing I might also mention that Pfänder's psychology does not exclude the unconscious, little though it mentions it. But Pfänder never defined the psyche as the conscious, much in the spirit of his teacher Theodor Lipps, whose plea for the unconscious was such valuable academic support to the cause of Sigmund Freud.

Thus Pfänder's descriptive psychology certainly satisfies the requirements of a phenomenological anthropology as far as man's experience of himself, his experiencing acts, and the experienced objects (body and world) are concerned. It fulfills it to a possibly even richer degree in his attempt to supply insights into essential structures, especially as he undertakes to determine the fundamental essence over and beyond the empirical data of the human psyche. Furthermore, with his attempt to understand the psychic life and the psyche itself as issuing from its fundamental essence, this psychology comes close not only to a genetic, as opposed to a static, phenomenology but also to a hermeneutic phenomenology which tries to interpret the more basic and less obvious features of human being in the world. Yet Pfänder always tries to submit his interpretations to phenomenological verification by intuitive demonstration based on examples from experience and free imaginative variation.

Pfänder also pays repeated and explicit attention to the way in which the world and the body are presented in our life as occupying a more or less extended place in it. These studies may well pass as attempts to show in what manner man is given to himself. To this extent Pfänder's psychology is also a phenomenology of the modes of appearance of man.

Only in one respect do I see a real gap in this psychology considered as a phenomenology of man: Pfänder does not discuss the question of how the phenomenon of man becomes constituted in his consciousness. How, for instance, does man's image of his own body or his self establish itself, how does it typically develop, become enriched or impoverished or otherwise modified? A complete phenomenology of man may well have something to say on these points. This would be the sort of constitution which Husserl had in mind when he spoke about the constitution of man's empirical ego in and by his transcendental ego. It could certainly be added to such a psychology, though it may not be needed by it for its own sake.

But then, how important and how fair would it be to make such demands on an enterprise which was not at all meant as a piece of phenomenological anthropology for its own sake as here outlined? Pfänder's interpretive psychology deserves to be studied on its own terms as an ambitious and fully-developed attempt to understand human life and the human psyche as an entity with an essential and understandable structure. If besides this primary goal it also fills the specifications of more recent demands, so much the better.

So my final plea is that the anthropology embodied in Pfänder's psychology be considered as an alternative to the conceptions of the more renowned philosophers, psychologists, and psychoanalysts. It is certainly much richer in phenomenological content, especially as far as the multiplicity of fundamental drives is concerned, compared with the one or two drives with which other systems operate. Economy is not its prime feature. But it does not abandon the search for a unifying understanding of variety. It avoids hypothetical constructions which can be verified only indirectly. Everywhere it tries to supply direct verification by phenomenological showing. It eschews, perhaps excessively, the discussion of rival theories. Some of its underlying conceptions, such as those of fundamental essences, may be in need of further explanation and examination. It is certainly too theoretical and complex for clinical and therapeutic applications. All that Pfänder offers in this regard is the concluding sentence of his brief preface:

> May this book help many people to better understand themselves and other human psyches, and may it besides find people to correct and to perfect it!

[*The following text is a translation of Pfänder's own announcement of his book on man's psyche, mentioned in the preceding article; the German original was never used and has not yet been published.*]

Translation of Author's Announcement

Pfänder, Alexander. *Man's Psyche. An Essay in Interpretive Psychology* (Halle, 1933).[7]

THIS BOOK has its origin in the deep disappointment which I experienced in the year 1893, when I became acquainted with so-called scientific psychology. Previously I had read with enthusiasm Schopenhauer and Nietzsche and expected to find in psychology something entirely different from what I was now offered. Even later I looked around in vain for the psychology I lacked. Gradually it became clear to me that I would have to make one of my own, if I did not want to go without one. However, the stage of psychology at that time made it very difficult to clarify even slightly what kind of psychology it was that I really wanted. There was no alternative to beginning, for the time being, with traditional psychology and trying to supplement and improve on it in the direction of the goal about which I was still in the dark. But on the sidelines I constantly made attempts, completely

7. In view of the different connotations in English and German, Pfänder's term *Seele* is here rendered not by "soul" but by the more neutral term "psyche." "Interpretive" is used for the German *verstehend* as most suggestive of what is involved: to provide the means for an understanding of the sense of the psyche. —Trans.

unconnected with the existing psychology, to penetrate into the minds of other people and into my own and to understand them as far as I could. I entertained the hope that an exploration of the real human psyche in daily life with as little bias as possible would eventually accumulate insights which, combined with the insights obtained through criticism of the prevailing psychology, would put me in a position to realize to some degree the ideal of my wishes. Not until the year 1913 did I succeed in forming a systematic whole out of what I had gradually attained, so that, in the summer of 1914, I could venture to present for the first time as a university lecture course the fundamental ideas of the present work under the title of "Fundamentals of the Psychology of Man" (*Grundzüge der Psychologie des Menschen*). I published parts of it in the treatise "Concerning the Psychology of Sentiments" ("Zur Psychologie der Gesinnungen") in the years 1913 and 1916,[8] other parts under the title "Fundamental Problems of Characterology" ("Grundprobleme der Charakterologie").[9] This psychology of man met with unexpectedly strong interest, but only at the beginning of the year 1930, when I believed I had reached the goal of my wishes, at least in its main outlines, could I make up my mind to give in to the urging of so many people to publish this psychology. Unfortunately, sickness delayed the completion of the work until the end of the year 1932.

From the outset the new title, *Man's Psyche*, points out several things: first, the fact that only psychology, not the anatomy and physiology of the sense organs, the nerves and the brain, is to be expected of this book; next, the fact that not only the life of the psyche but also and chiefly the psyche itself as a unitary living being is to be considered; and finally the fact that it is precisely the psyche of *man* in its peculiar nature which is to be the center of the investigation.

The subtitle "An Essay in Interpretive Psychology" (*verstehende Psychologie*) indicates that this is an attempt not only to know man's psyche and its life but also to understand it. No lengthy discussions of "understanding" (*verstehen*) and "interpretive psychology" (*verstehende Psychologie*) but interpretive psychological knowledge of the life of man's psyche and of the human psyche itself will be offered. This interpretive psychology is not to displace traditional psychology but to supplement it and in part to correct it. It is an "attempt" in the sense that it hopes for corrections and additions and would gladly welcome them.

The first part of the book has for its task the understanding of man's psychic life. To this end it offers first a systematic and wide survey of man's entire psychic life. In order to understand it, the purely psychic fundamental drives (*Grundtriebe*), not the somatic (*leiblich*) ones, are sought out, by which it is determined and controlled. Two groups of such fundamental drives are found in the human psyche, namely, drives that are directed toward something beyond one's own psyche and drives which refer to one's own psyche and its life. They are distinguished from each other as transitive and reflexive fundamental drives respectively. In each one of these two groups five different drives are identified. Next it is studied whether, how, and how far the life of the human psyche can be made intelligible from single drives, from groups of them, or from all of these drives together. It turns out that the life of the human psyche as it really is

8. E. Husserl, ed., *Jahrbuch für Philosophie und phänomenologische Forschung*, vols. I (1913), III (1916).

9. E. Utitz, ed., *Jahrbuch fur Charakterologie*, I (1924).

cannot be understood comprehensively nor with ultimate finality merely from these drives.

It proves necessary to go back to the essential nature of the human psyche and to recognize that it is permeated in a completely intelligible manner by a certain original drive (*Urtrieb*), namely, the drive toward progressive and stationary creative self-unfolding (*Selbstauszeugung*). Furthermore, it is discovered that this original drive of the human psyche contains in part all the previously identified drives and still other ones besides, in part makes them issue from itself in an intelligible manner. By going back to the original drive, which is intelligible by itself (*selbstverständlich*), the understanding of man's psychic life, as it was already attained from the functions of the fundamental drives, is enlarged, unified, and made more complete. However, difficulties of understanding result from the fact that most human psyches are externalized (*veräusserlicht*), that they behave in hostile fashion toward other beings, that they live their lives in estrangement from God, that they soon blindly try to remain just as they have come to be, that equally blindly they assimilate to people who surround them, and that they are overgrown by much that is fake and grafted on them. These difficulties are overcome by showing how, despite the presence of the original drive, a number of factors contribute in an intelligible manner to the result that men's psyches during their earthly lives usually more or less miss their original goal.

But the understanding of the human life thus attained is not yet completed, insofar as the goal of the original drive, namely, the human psyche in its full creative self-unfolding, is itself not yet sufficiently recognized and understood. The second part of this [second] book tries to supply this final completion of our understanding. Hence, it has to fulfill two tasks. First, it has to outline the idea of the human psyche, i.e., the human psyche as it would be in the state of complete creative self-unfolding. This is done in general and in detail by the method of "theoretical idealization" on the basis of factual experience, where, however, any idealization according to considerations of value is explicitly and strictly avoided.

But finally, the original goal of the human psyche must not only be recognized but also must be recognized as a meaningful goal. This is the second and last task of the second part of this book. It is not enough to recognize that the life in a fully self-unfolded human psyche is understandable, but this psyche itself must also be understood in a last and definitive manner. This is the result: the human psyche is not yet fully understandable in its idea by the fact that it is qualified for its own goals and for the goals of others, nor by the fact alone that it somehow is in accord with God's will, nor finally by the fact that it has particularly high value. In the last resort it is understandable only by the fact that all its parts, its organs, and its structure belong by intelligible necessity to its inmost essential nature, or, to put it differently, that as a human psyche it must exist on its own with full insight, in such shape as it really is when fully and creatively unfolded.

In the case of the human psyche, which strives for full creative self-unfolding in this earthly world, the idea of its goals assumes a specific, namely, the earthly shape. Not everything in this shape can be finally understood solely from the essential nature of the human psyche, but the fact, not per se understood, that in this world the psyche finds precisely this material and stands to it precisely in these (contingent) relations can be understood in part as responsible for its earthly shape.

Appendix B / "Linguistic Phenomenology": John L. Austin and Alexander Pfänder [1]

BY NOW it has become almost a cliché that Anglo-American and Continental European (including Ibero-American) philosophy are separated by a gulf, widest at the English Channel. Such clichés and the underlying metaphors of gulfs, curtains, and blocks can become dangerous once we become resigned to them.[2] But blocks can be broken up, curtains can be raised, and gulfs can be bridged. My preference is for trying to build bridges.

It seems to me that the Spanish-American world offers an unusually good setting for building another such bridge. For, probably thanks to Ortega y Gasset, Spanish philosophy has been particularly hospitable not only to the phenomenologists and existential philosophers most popular in France and Italy, such as Husserl, Scheler, and Heidegger, but also to the less spectacular work of the Munich phenomenologist Alexander Pfänder, whose *Phenomenology of Willing* and *Logic* were translated into Spanish in the early thirties. Even more pertinent, his *Logic*, the translation of which has gone through several editions, has been put to productive use here in Mexico in the philosophy of law of Eduardo García Máynez. Thus here in Mexico the choice of Pfänder's phenomenology as one of the abutments of the new bridge needs no lengthy justification.

The other abutment will be more familiar, especially among Anglo-American philosophers. Although John L. Austin was not the lead-

1. This paper, presented by Herbert Spiegelberg, was originally published in *Memorias del XII Congreso Internacional de Filosofía*, IX (1964), 509–17, and is reprinted with the permission of the Universidad Nacional Autónoma de México.

2. Among those who have resigned prematurely I suspect the editor of the recent Colloque de Royaumont on *La Philosophie analytique* (Paris, 1962), Leslie Beck, whose *Avant-Propos* expresses serious doubt about the success of this particular dialogue. But his own evidence is hardly that discouraging. Thus he tells us that "when Merleau-Ponty asked 'Isn't our program the same?' the firm and clean-cut answer (of Gilbert Ryle) was 'I hope not.'" But if one looks up the printed record, the only place where this answer occurs is in reply to Merleau-Ponty's question of whether Ryle in his studies was always "in strict accord with the program outlined at the beginning of the century by Russell and refined by Wittgenstein and some others" (p. 98). Austin, who took a leading part in the discussion, was perhaps even more conciliatory than Ryle, again judging from the published text of the proceedings.

ing figure among the Oxford analysts, recent publications from his posthumous papers and lectures reveal the gravity of his untimely loss, not only to British philosophy but to the world at large.

But these circumstances do not yet justify my linking the names of the English analyst and the much older Munich phenomenologist. Indeed it is more than unlikely that either one knew of the other even by name. The sole justification for mentioning them in one breath is the unconscious convergence of their ideas. In fact, as far as Pfänder is concerned, this convergence can be shown only on the basis of posthumous material, of which very little has been published thus far.[3]

Nevertheless, I believe it can be shown that Austin's type of analysis was moving beyond mere linguistic analysis toward a supplementary study of the phenomena which led very close to an explicit phenomenology. From the other side Pfänder, who did not formulate his conception of phenomenology until late in his career, came to realize that phenomenology proper presupposes a conceptual analysis under the name of "clarification of meaning (*Sinnklärung*)," to be guided largely by what we mean by the terms of our ordinary language. It is not my contention that the completion of Austin's and Pfänder's enterprises would have resulted in a dovetailing bridge. Between the approaches of two philosophers so different in background and development there remain important differences, which I do not want to gloss over. But I believe that here are two forms of analytic philosophy and phenomenology which are not only congenial but which, fully developed, could complement one another.

In order to show this incipient convergence I shall first trace the trend toward phenomenology in Austin. The most explicit expression of this trend can be found in his Presidential Address to the Aristotelian Society in 1957,[4] which contains the following paragraph:

> In view of the prevalence of the slogan "ordinary language" and of such names as "linguistic" or "analytic" philosophy or "the analysis of language," one thing needs special emphasis in order to counter misunderstandings. When we examine what we should say when, what words we should use in what situations, we are looking again not *merely* at words (or "meanings," whatever they may be) but also at the realities we use the words to talk about: we are using a sharpened awareness of words to sharpen our perception of, though not as the final arbiter of, the phenomena. For this reason I think it might be better to use, for this way of doing philosophy, some less misleading name than those given above—for instance, "linguistic phenomenology," only that is rather a mouthful (p. 8).

On the strength of this statement one might well suspect that at this point Austin felt actually closer to phenomenology than to "linguistics." Even the fact that in the new hybrid expression "phenomenology" and not "linguistics" is the noun might indicate this. Also, the text makes it plain that the study of linguistics is to serve as a means to "sharpen our perception of the phenomena." That this is his ulti-

---

3. See Herbert Spiegelberg, *Alexander Pfänder's Phänomenologie* (The Hague, 1963), Appendix.

4. "A Plea for Excuses," *Proceedings of the Aristotelian Society*, LVII (1957), 1–30; also in *Philosophical Papers* (Oxford, 1961), p. 130.

mate objective was spelled out even more fully when Austin answered
H. L. Van Breda's questions at the Colloque de Royaumont as
follows:

> We use the multiplicity of expressions which the richness of our lan-
> guage furnishes us in order to direct our attention to the multiplicity
> and the richness of our experiences. Language serves us as interpreter
> for observing the living facts which constitute our experience, which,
> without it, we would tend to overlook . . . The diversity of expressions
> which we can apply attracts our attention to the extraordinary com-
> plexity of the situations on which we are called upon to speak. This
> means that language illumines for us the complexity of life.[5]

However, this does not yet mean that Austin's "phenomenology"
deals directly with the phenomena rather than with the expressions
that lead to them. In fact, even at Royaumont Austin's answer seems
to have sidestepped Van Breda's double question: "To what degree do
we make use of criteria which are not strictly linguistic? In what
measure do we study phenomena which are not strictly phenomena of
language when we go beyond the point at which we have arrived thus
far?" No extra-linguistic criteria are explicitly admitted or denied. The
only avenue to the phenomena considered seems to be that through
language.

All that can be maintained on the basis of the paragraph in the
Presidential Address is, therefore, that Austin contemplated a change
in name for his analysis of language in view of its ultimate objective.
No direct study of the phenomena is as yet at stake. In particular,
there is no evidence that Austin was interested in phenomenology in a
technical and especially in the Continental sense of the term. His
aversion to the "mouthful" of as clumsy a hybrid as "linguistic phenomenology" may therefore reflect more than the new Oxford purism,
namely, a shying away from suspicious allies, especially those using
technical jargon, like the Continental phenomenologists.

However, the decisive question is whether Austin's way of doing
philosophy has genuine affinity with what phenomenologists do. Stuart
Hampshire in his memorial for Austin [6] distinguishes between a
stronger and a weaker thesis implied in Austin's way of doing philosophy. The stronger is to the effect that "for every distinction of word
and idiom that we find in common speech, there is a reason to be
found, if we look far enough, to explain why this distinction exists" (p.
iii). Language, as Wittgenstein had put it, is always "in order as it is,"
and if we only study it painstakingly, it will yield all the relevant
information about the world in all its intricacy. Austin's posthumously
published lectures on *Sense and Sensibilia* provide one of the best
examples of this procedure. The weaker thesis, as Hampshire states it,
merely implies that "we must first have the facts, and all the facts (of
the existing distinctions marked in common speech) accurately stated,
before we erect a theory upon the basis of them" (p. vi). Austin
maintained that the neglect of this prime prerequisite was at the root
of the "scandal" that philosophy has remained so inconclusive. However, the inventory thus to be collected would supply merely the
"indispensable *preliminary* to any philosophical advance" (p. ix). This

---

5. *La Philosophie analytique*, p. 333.
6. "In Memoriam J. L. Austin 1911–1960," *Proceedings of the Aristotelian
Society*, LX (1960), i–xiv.

clearly suggests that it would have to be followed up by the study of the facts.

Austin's explicit reflections about his own method, especially those in his Presidential Address, seem to me to keep much closer to the weaker thesis. This becomes clearest from his discussion of the alleged "snag" for linguistic philosophy called the "crux of the last word," about which Austin has this to say:

> Certainly ordinary language has no claim to be the last word, if there is such a thing . . . In principle it can everywhere be supplemented and improved upon and superseded. Only remember, it *is* the *first* word.[7]

This may suggest that already the second word of philosophy is no longer linguistic analysis. In any case, the last word would belong to a study of the phenomena to which the linguistic expressions refer. In fact, it would seem that the study of the phenomena would have to enter in at least two ways: first, in the sense of the phenomena such as they are envisioned by ordinary language; second, in the sense of the phenomena as they emerge from a fresh examination of the facts, either by science or by some other direct approach, such as phenomenology in the continental sense. In the light of this second exploration ordinary language and its picture of the phenomena may prove to be inadequate and even wrong.

But while this phenomenological extension of linguistic analysis is clearly foreshadowed, Austin himself does not seem to have undertaken it. Thus his "plea for excuses," one of the most brilliant demonstrations of his linguistic perceptiveness, does not yet advance beyond a painstaking review of the language of excuses.

Now for the opposite picture of Pfänder's phenomenology and its stake in linguistic analysis.

It must be realized that, in spite of Pfänder's key role in the growth of the original Phenomenological Movement and especially of its Munich branch, he was rather slow in formulating his theoretical conception of phenomenology, and particularly in stating it in print. His early use of the term, actually even before Husserl, in his *Phänomenologie des Wollens* of 1901, designates not much more than a descriptive psychology, and even his much more brilliant "Psychologie der Gesinnungen" in the first and third volumes of Husserl's *Jahrbuch* of 1913 and 1916 is mainly another example of such a phenomenological psychology with special emphasis on the need of determining the essences of the empirical facts. In his *Logic* of 1921, the development of Husserl's original program of a pure logic freed from psychologism, he is strangely non-committal about the question of what phenomenology really is.

> To state briefly and yet intelligibly what phenomenology is and is striving for today is a request coming from many quarters, but at the moment it is hardly possible to fulfill it. All that can be done is to give some hints as to the subject and the task of phenomenology and to characterize the position of logic in relation to the science so characterized.[8]

7. *Ibid.*, LVII (1957), 11; *Philosophical Papers*, p. 132.
8. *Logik* (Halle, 1921), p. 33; see above, p. 66.

This statement is followed by a half-page which characterizes phenomenology as the viewing of the world from the perspective of the subject, the attempt to study the ideas and beliefs of this subject by describing its intentional objects as well as its intentional acts, and furthermore the modes of givenness of these objects and the modes of these acts. Since pure logic as it is studied in the *Logik* is not found to be dependent on such a phenomenology, no further discussion or illustration of this conception follows in the text.

Pfänder had no chance to state his fully-developed conception of phenomenology in print, a conception which differed considerably from Husserl's parallel conceptions. All the more important is it to point out that it was Pfänder's definite plan to round up his work with the publication not only of an *Ethics* but also of an *Introduction to Philosophy;* the latter was at the same time to serve as an introduction to his mature phenomenology, for which he also used the name "Munich phenomenology," clearly in order to distinguish it from Husserl's Freiburg phenomenology. In fact, the course of lectures which was to be the foundation for that book and which Pfänder offered sixteen times during his years of teaching finally went by the title of "Introduction to Philosophy *and Phenomenology."* But Pfänder's growing heart ailment prevented him from carrying out his plan beyond a few introductory fragments. Thus the only authentic source for a reconstruction of this phenomenology is his careful lecture notes, which, however, do not form a continuous text, but consist only of key sentences.[9] Yet they are sufficient for forming a clear idea of his conception and its intended development. The problem of how to edit them remains to be solved. But even now it is possible and defensible to describe the general structure of this phenomenology and particularly those features of it which resemble Austin's "linguistic phenomenology."

The general plan of Pfänder's *Introduction* consists in the successive examination of the major substantive problems of philosophy, such as the nature of the inanimate world, of life, of the psyche, of values, and of ideal demands. In each case Pfänder first discusses the opposite approaches of rationalism, empiricism, and Kantian Critical philosophy to these problems, in order to introduce phenomenology as the solution to the deadlock caused by their failures. The major symptom of these failures is the falsifications and misinterpretations of the original phenomena to which these approaches had to resort. Any attempt to do justice to the phenomena has, therefore, to begin with a removal of these misconstructions and with the recovery of the original phenomena and the genuine issues.

Apparently, in introducing phenomenology as a fourth way by invoking the authentic phenomena, Pfänder became more and more aware of the necessity of first clearing the ground by restoring the original sense of the problems at stake. Thus his method as he finally worked it out consisted of three distinct steps:

(1) clarification of meaning (*Sinnklärung*) aiming at the elucidation of what we really mean;

(2) "*epoché*," a term obviously taken over from Husserl, implying for Pfänder simply the neutralizing suspension of belief in the existence of what is meant, aiming at blocking the tendency to infer from the fact of our meaning the existence of its referent;

9. A preview of this conception is contained in the text translated in chap. 4 of this volume.

(3) phenomenology of perception or perceptual verification of our clarified and neutralized meanings, sometimes also called "phenomenology proper," aiming at the determination of whether our meanings are justified in the light of the phenomena to which they point.

In this context I shall not discuss this three-step method, its rights and limitations, in its entirety. Instead I shall focus on the first step, the clarification of meaning as the possible equivalent of "linguistic phenomenology." What exactly is involved in Pfänder's "clarification of meaning"? As a representative example of it I shall use his analysis of "what is meant by a material object (*Körper*)." Here Pfänder first points out negatively that we mean by it not one sense datum or an aggregate of many sense data, not a concept, and not something unknown behind the sense data. Then he determines positively that what is really meant is an extended, space-occupying piece of material. The same procedure is followed with regard to the meaning of its properties (*Eigenschaften*) and to the ways in which we mean these properties to be related to the material thing. Besides, Pfänder examines what we mean by the perception of such bodies.

To what extent can such a clarification of meaning be considered linguistic analysis? Certainly Pfänder does not speak explicitly about analyzing *word* meanings. Nor does he use inverted commas or mention language as such. The emphasis is clearly on identifying and describing the referents of our thinking and speaking. On the other hand, the formulation "What is meant by . . . ?" which occurs over and over again in Pfänder's text makes it plain that this analysis takes its departure from the word "body" as it is commonly used. In fact, since Pfänder often asks "What do *we* mean?" there can be little doubt that his primary goal is to make sure of the ordinary meaning of these terms by establishing the referents to which they ordinarily point. Now the above example, the first in Pfänder's text, gives certainly no evidence of detailed study of, or special interest in, the nuances and shadings of ordinary language. It should be pointed out, however, that when Pfänder criticizes the poverty of the current theories of value, he collects carefully the variety of appraising predicates in everyday use, such as the German equivalents of "pretty" (*hübsch*), "dainty" (*niedlich*), "delicate" (*zierlich*), "nice" (*nett*), etc. Thus Pfänder is well aware of the fact that ordinary language is the depository of a wealth of meaning all too easily overlooked and that it should be consulted first and foremost if we don't want to miss the phenomena as meant.

Pfänder's clarification of meaning was thus certainly not a full-fledged counterpart of Austin's linguistic analysis. It lacks the painstaking subtlety of his procedures and reports. But it clearly acknowledges the need for such analysis in the case of the major philosophical problems. It emphasizes less than Austin the linguistic expressions and uses them merely as springboards for exploring our meanings, which need not always be put in words. This may have the advantage that such an analysis is not dependent on the peculiarities of any particular language at a particular stage of its historical development. For this can easily become one of the pitfalls of a linguistic analysis which depends on one specific language such as the king's English.

Besides, Pfänder's second step, the suspension of belief, should immunize his analysis of meanings from the dangers of the well-known semantic fallacy of inferring from the word to the existence of the thing, which Austin's "strong thesis" might easily promote. Austin himself was certainly on his guard against this danger. It seems worth pointing out that in leaning over backward from it, he came very close to the phenomenological *epoché*.[10] The real test for the entire method could come, of course, only with the third step of phenomenology proper or phenomenology of perception. It involved a fresh start by a direct approach to the phenomena, about which much more would have to be said but which clearly is not matched in Austin's actual procedure.

What, then, is the upshot of this seemingly far-fetched confrontation of two historically unrelated philosophers? As far as Austin is concerned, I submit that there is concrete evidence that Austin, quite apart from his coining and nearly adopting the phrase "linguistic phenomenology," was headed beyond mere linguistic analysis toward an examination of the phenomena to which language refers. But he seems to have considered linguistic analysis the indispensable preparation for it, and does not seem to have envisaged a direct approach to the phenomena as a feasible alternative.

As far as Pfänder was concerned, he did add an extension to his phenomenology, namely, a preparatory or propaedeutic phase of analysis of meanings, including linguistic meanings, to precede phenomenology, which was his primary concern. True, what we find even in his unpublished texts cannot compare with the refinement of Austin's analyses. Also, it is not clear how far he considered analysis of meanings an indispensable step for phenomenology. But he clearly implied that in the area of the major philosophical problems which had undergone the distorting influence of pre-phenomenological philosophies a semantic and linguistic purge was the proper preparation for a fresh start.

I maintain, then, that in the case of Austin and Pfänder analysis and phenomenology converged, linguistic analysis pointing beyond itself to a correlated study of the phenomena, phenomenology discovering the usefulness of a preparatory study of ordinary meanings. This does not mean that the two opposite extensions of these philosophies can be put together and riveted into a solid bridge. But it suggests at least that developments from both sides properly correlated can be used for working cooperatively on the same problems from different directions. This is in fact what I should like to suggest in conclusion: in certain areas of philosophy, particularly those which have already come under the cultivation of ordinary language, a two-pronged approach is not only *possible*, it promises mutual stimulation and verification. Linguistic analysis can sharpen our eyes for shades in the phenomena for which our individual phenomenological eyes are not yet sufficiently sensitized. Phenomenology can clear the ground for the verification of the distinctions of ordinary language and at the same time make room for its orderly development beyond its present stage. There is no need for an either-or. Analysis as well as phenomenology stands to benefit from a both-and.

10. See his Presidential Address, *Proceedings of the Aristotelian Society*, LXII (1957), 11 n.5: "And forget for once and for a while, that other curious question, 'Is it true? May we?'"

Bibliography

THERE WOULD BE little point in adding here a complete bibliography of the entire literature dealing with Pfänder. I shall confine myself to a chronological list of Pfänder's own writings and to the English literature about him. A list of German secondary literature will be found in my book, *Alexander Pfänder's Phänomenologie* (The Hague, 1963), p. 71.

PFÄNDER'S WRITINGS

1898   "Das Bewusstsein des Wollens," *Zeitschrift für Psychologie und Physiologie der Sinnesorgane*, XVII, 521–67.
Review of GEORG HEIGEL, "Versuch einer Lösung des Willensproblems," *ibid.*, pp. 465 f.

1899   Review of HUGO MÜNSTERBERG, "The Psychology of the Will," *ibid.*, XXI, 302 ff.

1900   *Phänomenologie des Wollens. Eine psychologische Analyse.* Leipzig, Johann Ambrosius Barth. (3rd ed.; 1963.)
Review of W. WEYGANDT, "Römers Versuche über Nahrungsaufnahme und geistige Leistungsfähigkeit," *Zeitschrift für Psychologie und Physiologie der Sinnesorgane*, XXIII, 143 f.
Review of G. F. STOUT, "A Manual of Psychology," *ibid.*, pp. 415–19.

1904   *Einführung in die Psychologie.* Leipzig, Johann Ambrosius Barth.

1911   "Vorwort des Herausgebers," *Münchener Philosophische Abhandlungen.* Theodor Lipps zu seinem sechzigsten Geburtstag gewidmet von früheren Schülern. Leipzig, Johann Ambrosius Barth. Pp. iii f.
"Motive und Motivation," *ibid.*, pp. 163–95.

[93]

"Nietzsche," *Grosse Denker*, ed. V. ASTER. Leipzig, Quelle & Meyer. Vol. II, 331–60. (Revised 2d ed.; 1923, pp. 356–86.)

1913 "Zur Psychologie der Gesinnungen," Part I, *Jahrbuch für Philosophie und phänomenologische Forschung*, I, 325–404.

1916 "Zur Psychologie der Gesinnungen," Part II, *ibid.*, III, 1–125.

1920 *Einführung in die Psychologie*. Leipzig, Johann Ambrosius Barth. Revised 2d ed.

1921 "Logik," *Jahrbuch für Philosophie und phänomenologische Forschung*, IV, 139–499. (3rd ed.; Tübingen, Max Niemeyer Verlag, 1963.)

1924 "Grundprobleme der Charakterologie," *Jahrbuch der Charakterologie*, ed. E. Utitz, I, 289–355.

1928 Review of KURT STAVENHAGEN, *Absolute Stellungnahmen*, in *Zeitwende*, IV, 287 f.

1929 Review of THEODOR CELMS, *Der phänomenologische Idealisms Husserls*, in *Deutsche Literaturzeitung*, L, 2048–50.

1930 Combined reprint of *Phänomenologie des Wollens* and "Motive und Motivation." Leipzig, Johann Ambrosius Barth.

1933 *Die Seele des Menschen*. Versuch einer verstehenden Psychologie. Halle, Max Niemeyer Verlag.

1948 *Philosophie der Lebensziele*, ed. posthumously by WOLFGANG TRILLHAAS. Göttingen, Vandenhoeck & Rupprecht. (Lecture course given in the Winter semester, 1921–22. According to the editor, these lecture notes taken by Ernst Heller and Anna Dietz had been "corrected and in places even supplemented from the first to the last page by Pfänder himself." The original manuscript no longer exists.)

PFÄNDERIANA

SINCE 1953, Pfänder's philosophical papers, consisting of 114 entries, have been kept in the Manuscript Division of the Bayerische Staatsbibliothek in Munich.

LITERATURE IN ENGLISH

1. Anonymous review of *Einführung in die Psychologie*, in *Mind*, XIII (1904), 579–80. "We do not know of any other book which fulfills the same function as the *Einführung*. Dr. Pfänder has done well a piece for which there was great need."

2. BOSENQUET, BERNARD. Review of *Jahrbuch für Philosophie und*

phänomenologische Forschung, I (1913) in *Mind*, XXIII (1914), 591 f. including "Zur Psychologie der Gesinnungen," Part I.
"The spirit and thoroughness of the attempt are excellent; and the fact that I cannot recognize the aptness of all the above descriptive phrases may be due to my defects rather than theirs."

3. JONES, TUDOR. *Contemporary Thoughts of Germany*. London, William & Norgate, 1931, II, 113–16. Jones devotes a special section of his chapter on Phenomenology to Pfänder. While on the whole very appreciative of his importance, Jones misunderstands basic features of his logic and psychology, as far as he reports about them.

4. LAIRD, JOHN. *Recent Philosophy*. London, T. Butterworth, Ltd., 1936. While Pfänder figures correctly among the contributors to Husserl's yearbook and even as a pioneer of phenomenology, he is mentioned misleadingly as a supporter of Alexius Meinong (p. 118) and in a chapter on "The New Medievalism," in the wake of Scheler, as "A phenomenological Neo-Thomist," an odd label for the Protestant Pfänder.

5. SPIEGELBERG, HERBERT. "Alexander Pfänder 1870–1941," *Philosophy and Phenomenological Research*, II (1941), 263–65.

6. ————. Review of ALEXANDER PFÄNDER, *Philosophie der Lebensziele, ibid.*, X (1949), 438–42.

7. ————. *The Phenomenological Movement*. The Hague, Martinus Nijhoff. 2d ed., 1965, pp. 173–92.

8. ————. "'Linguistic Phenomenology': John L. Austin and Alexander Pfänder." See Appendix B, pp. 86–92.

9. ————. "The Idea of a Phenomenological Anthropology and Alexander Pfänder's Psychology of Man." See Appendix A, pp. 75–85.

10. SOKOLOWSKI, ROBERT. Review of recent Pfänder publications in *The Modern Schoolman*, XLIII (1966), 292–95.

Index

NAMES

Aristotle, 42
Austin, John L., xxvi, 86–92

Beck, Leslie, 86 n
Binswanger, Ludwig, 32, 79, 80
Breda, H. L. Van, 88
Brentano, Franz, 4, 70
Buytendijk, F. J. J., 80

Descartes, René, 71

Frege, Gottlob, 41
Freud, Sigmund, 82

García Máynez, Eduardo, 86
Gebsattel, Viktor von, 80
Geiger, Moritz, xviii

Hampshire, Stuart, 88
Hartmann, Nicolai, xviii
Hehlmann, Wilhelm, 13
Heidegger, Martin, xvii, xix, xxi, 79
Hengstenberg, Hans-Edward, 79
Hume, David, 72
Husserl, Edmund, xv, xvi, xix, 4, 41,
    43, 57, 60, 71, 76, 79

James, William, 3
Janet, Pierre, 13

Kaam, Adrian van, xi, xvi, 80
Kant, Immanuel, xxii, 21, 53, 72
Külpe, Oswald, 3

Leyendecker, Herbert, xviii
Lipps, Theodor, xvi, 13, 17, 23 n,
    28, 82

Locke, John, 72

McClellan, David, 13
Marcel, Gabriel, 79
May, Rollo, 80
Meinong, Alexius, xviii, 4
Merleau-Ponty, Maurice, 79, 86 n
Minkowski, Eugène, 80
Müller, Karl Alexander von, xviii
Münsterberg, Hugo, 3

Nietzsche, Friedrich, xvi, xxi, 83

Ortega y Gasset, José, 81, 86

Peters, R. S., 13

Reinach, Adolf, xviii
Ribot, Théodule, 3
Ricoeur, Paul, xv, 12
Russell, Bertrand, 41, 86 n
Ryle, Gilbert, 4, 86 n

Sartre, Jean-Paul, 13 n
Scheler, Max, xvii, xviii, xix, 76, 78
Schopenhauer, Arthur, xvi, xxi, 53,
    83
Schröder, Eduard, 41
Schütz, Alfred, 14
Sigwart, Christoph, 41
Straus, Erwin, 80

Teilhard de Chardin, Pierre, 77, 78
Thomsen, Andreas, 15

Wittgenstein, Ludwig, 41, 86 n, 88
Wundt, Wilhelm, 3

SUBJECTS